PAX EVAN
TIBI GELI
MAR STA
CE MEVS

Venezia

'SO MUCH HAS BEEN SAID AND WRITTEN ABOUT VENICE
THAT IT APPEARS TO ME THERE IS NOTHING LEFT TO SAY.'

CANON PIETRO CASOLA – 1494

VENEZIA

BY

SERGE SIMONART

An evocative and atmospheric photo book, brimming with antiquarian treasures and historic Venetian ephemera. A volume to lose yourself in.

First Edition

HANNIBAL

—

2020

bile Da S:
Alla Croce

LA

SERENISSIMA

Gustav von Aschenbach
was right: "Arriving in
Venice
from the train station
was like entering a palace
through the servants' entrance…
one should always, like himself,
travel across the ocean to this most
improbable of cities."
Although the night train also has
its charms: to open your eyes in
the morning is to imagine yourself
in heaven. As if you are stepping inside
a painting by Canaletto. As if the
whole city is rendered in trompe l'oeil.
As if Atlantis has risen.

Inclita regina uergene poncella
Del mondo ſpechio ſei Venetia bella.

Venice is an aberration, an anachronism, an open-air museum, a ghost town, a film set, a miracle, an out-of-control experiment by an enigmatic alchemist-cum-architect. No other city on earth is all those things. § Venice is a maze, a labyrinth designed by a decadent eccentric; a mystical vision of crystallised melancholy; the mythical backdrop to a daily operatic performance in which only the extras come and go – and where courtesans in sweeping gowns once strolled with parasols in their hands, girls in low-rise jeans now amble around while glued to their iPads. § As a child, I believed that Venice was a migratory, floating city that would wash up on one shore and then on another. On my first visit to Venice, I was staggered by how near it was, how reachable, and I questioned my right to even be there – was I entitled to experience this level of beauty, could one enjoy it with impunity? I could not believe it existed, but nor could I believe that it had not *always* existed.

Venice is petrified beauty, a fossil, a formation of giant stalagmites. After all these years, and despite the crowds, Venice is still *terra incognita*, a Sleeping Beauty, a hidden treasure. You conduct ground-level archaeology: as though you are unlocking long-forgotten secrets in every street, simply by looking around. It is hard to resist the urge to hunt for a golden *zecchino* or a lost seventeenth-century manuscript behind every gate, in every alcove, under every beam. § Majestic decay is the norm here – the pockmarked, crumbled and weathered *palazzi* are not an act of surrender but a triumph, an aesthetic orgasm, the sublime patina of the city. Anything that is not ruinously eroded, oxidised or battered seems wholly out of place. Just by never changing, Venice resists the feverish zeitgeist. § No two houses are identical here, yet Venice is a harmonious whole. Nowhere else do past and present fuse so seamlessly. Nowhere else does history seem quite so tangible: courtesans, dukes and Marco Polo await *dietro le quinte*, and was that shadow not Casanova? If Leonardo da Vinci were to rise from the grave and visit contemporary Venice, then he would recognise almost everything.

In summer, the shimmering light turns Venice into a mirage. Yet you can be swallowed up by the shadows the moment you cross a bridge. The real Venice can be discovered during its hibernation period, those months in which the mist, fog, cold and *acqua alta* intensify its self-imposed isolation. § Venice exudes grandeur whilst also inspiring delusions of grandeur – you are tempted to assume a sense of *grandezza*, to adopt a slightly more regal bearing than is strictly necessary and to add the prefix Chevalier to your name. But rather a pauper in Venice than a king anywhere else.

“Venice is a cliché, a Renaissance Disneyland befitting a chocolate box,” say the sceptics. A cliché, yes, but then so are the *St Matthew Passion* and *A Little Night Music*. And Mahler’s *Adagietto* has been ubiquitous since *Death in Venice*. Should they all be abolished? If an artwork is hijacked by slick opportunists, or simple souls fail to look (or listen) beyond the most superficial layers of a painting or musical score, it does not mean there is something inherently wrong with the works in question. Mass production and mass tourism will never diminish the uniqueness and significance of Venice. Those who regard the city as the ultimate cliché have lost their capacity for wonder; they would undoubtedly view cherry blossom with suspicion and judge the sincerest emotions to be false. A friend’s father had one abiding memory of Venice: “it stank”. Such people might well be my compatriots, but they inhabit a different planet. I refuse to become a blasé cynic who derives no pleasure from a sunset because it has already been reproduced on a zillion postcards. If you cannot rhapsodise about Venice, then what can you? This is the last place in the world that one should contemplate in cool and rational terms.

As you sail out into the lagoon, towards the modern world and Mestre, the ugliness starts to accumulate. Compared to Venice, many other cities seem derailed, misguided. If Monte Carlo and Dubai are the whores of the nouveau riche, then La Serenissima is a venerable, eternally proud and elegant dowager duchess. She can count on my unwavering esteem and devotion. She has stood her ground. The guild of real-estate opportunists has yet to establish a foothold in Venice. Here, the egos of modern architects who want to commit patricide against their Renaissance colleagues are crushed by a single, sacred principle: one cannot demolish a jewel from 1432, 1648 or 1792 and replace it with a concrete monstrosity. Despite its age, this magical city seems to be a dowry that has been bequeathed to humanity by a higher life form. § When the world ran amok, someone forgot to tell Venice. Here, you can escape the tyranny of always aspiring to be the Newest, Fastest, Highest. It is an oasis of centuries-old wood, marble and stone in a world of concrete, plastic and steel. Contemporary humanity is orphaned and uprooted, and we instinctively know that a postmodern skyscraper provides little in the way of nourishment. Is this not one of the reasons why so many visitors flock to Venice? Because people are unconsciously striving to get away from it all and decontaminate themselves? Because they long for a city without building violations, potholes, billboards and other forms of visual pollution? Despite its decay, the city of the Doges pulls the brake on transience. Venice's relative immutability provides solace to modern mankind, to all those who are cast adrift and floundering. For those who crave beauty, purity and authenticity, Venice is a moral compass. § After all, it is more than just a city: Venice is a state of mind, the essence of life, a sanctuary for dreamers, a spiritual spa, a sanatorium for wounded angels. § There are two kinds of people. Firstly, the vampires: those who see Venice as nothing more than the idyllic backdrop to their own navel-gazing activities, the day-trippers and other misfits for whom the city is a mere pawn on their chessboards. These are the people who tarnish Venice with their presence. Secondly, the devotees: those who make pilgrimages to Venice, who worship the sacred city and pay it homage, if only by choosing not to litter the streets, to speak in hushed tones and to learn a smattering of Italian as a gesture of goodwill. § Out of season, when the city's heartbeat is no longer muffled by the sound of braying tourists, I feel as though we might all be uprooted Venetians in exile, kindred spirits, people who have finally returned home after a meandering Grand Tour. § Who has not thought: I could live here? But which is better: living in Venice as an immigrant or treating yourself to regular visits to this paradise?

I can read the irritation in the eyes of certain Venetians, the sense that they have reached saturation point. I prefer to avoid Stendhal's syndrome: I do not want to become immune to beauty, nor succumb to a fatal overdose. So I visit Venice often, yet also as seldom as possible. Fortunately, Venice has a long half-life: a visit stays with you for ages. And like Proust (also a devoted temporary Venetian) with his madeleines, even an incident of light or a weathered block of marble, when seen in a horrid place like Chernobyl, can evoke Venice. But if my soul has a different address to my body, then that address is Venice. § And there is beauty to be found in the city at various stages of life and with different companions, such as the Muse who first arrived here as Alma Mahler, later as Alma Werfel and Alma Kokoschka, and even later as *The Merry Widow*. Or like Giacomo Casanova, who saw his hometown as a child, as a patrician, as the arch-seducer, as a prisoner and as an exile... but never as an old man.

Every day, a first-time visitor to Venice will enquire about the most direct route to his or her hotel. "The shortest or the most beautiful?" I once overheard the concierge at the Hotel Des Bains respond. The tourist who chose the most beautiful route is still wandering the streets. Getting lost is one of the most wonderful things you could wish for in Venice. I hope you will regularly lose yourself in the pages of this book. Being lost is very *Venezianissimo.*

PERDERSI A VENEZIA

Open my heart and you will see, graved inside of it, 'Italy'", wrote the English poet Robert Browning, who died at the Ca'Rezzonico in 1889. Replace Italy with Venice, and you have my own personal motto. Venice is not just another city, it is a place in which a feeling for life is crystallised, and in this sense it is the antithesis of, say, Manhattan. § Let me tell you what happened on the very first day of my inaugural visit to Venice: I was standing in a street of a certain district, glanced up at a tower and a section of wall and suddenly realised – I am lost. No city is more delightful to be lost in than Venice. To be more precise: losing your way here is a privilege. Should it happen to you, then enjoy the experience. And because Venice is a relatively small and safe peninsula, not to mention traffic free, the best of both worlds can be guaranteed: disorientation and risk-free wandering while secure in the knowledge that you will get there in the end. In around 1900, Marcel Proust, who said of his lengthy stay in Venice, "my dream became my address", kept notes about all the little patches of *terra incognita*, alleyways and tiny squares that were missing from his plan of Venice. Even today, Venice is an illogical city, one in which house numbers are sometimes missing or can even be wrong, but that too is pure poetry. § People who claim that Venice is expensive ought to enjoy more of the free (yet priceless) attractions that the city has to offer. Getting lost in Venice is just one of them. It is best to do this at sunrise (the early bird catches more than the worm in Venice) or sundown, or in other words, when the invasion of day-trippers has not yet commenced or has petered out. The city is rarely or never empty, except for a few weeks in November or January. As early as the eighteenth century, the death of a Doge was concealed for three weeks "so as not to harm the tourist season". Tourism in Venice no longer knows a lull, but it does have an ebb and flow. Lingering by the Rialto Bridge in high summer is like visiting the Vatican after the cesspit has just been drained. § If you think that an espresso on the terraces of Caffè Florian or Caffè Quadri is overpriced, perhaps you have forgotten the accompanying orchestra and incomparable panorama that come for free. Nowhere else are there so many priceless things that cost nothing. Do not be a cheapskate when you arrive in Venice. Seeing this beautiful city for the first time is a once-in-a-lifetime experience. Invest in a water taxi that will collect you from the airport and ferry you graciously across the lagoon, thus enabling you to behold the silhouette of La Serenissima rising up from the mist and to glide along the Grand Canal as though floating into an open-air museum on a magic carpet. The only valid alternative is to arrive at the nineteenth-century station via the night train. You are thrown headlong into the city as soon as you exit the terminus – an experience that is only comparable to a curtain being lifted on a decadent opera performance. Hire a relatively affordable gondola too (if only you knew how expensive these vessels are to buy and maintain, and how physically gruelling to operate) and cruise through the quiet side canals of Dorsoduro or Cannaregio during off-peak hours, preferably around midnight, which is the best way to imagine yourself in 1697.

Only characterless souls who are missing the melancholy gene will complain about the rain or cold in Venice, for this is a fairy-tale city that divulges different secrets according to the myriad atmospheric conditions. Bad weather only enhances the mystique of Venice; in this city, what was previously an *eau de toilette* becomes a *parfum*. Nowhere are the rain-drenched facades more beautiful. Nowhere else does snow seem more of a blessing than a curse. Nowhere is the mist, fog and dusk more mysterious than here, for they seem to be allies, or even patrons, of the city. The surface of the Grand Canal is like a mirror that has been weathered by time, gnawed at by fog. Richard Wagner travelled to Venice in search of fine weather. It turned out to be dismal, but the grey melancholy of La Serenissima merged with his own innate desolation, and it is to this we owe *Tristan and Isolde.*

Venice is the aesthetic focal point of Western history, the heart and soul of the civilised world, the *nec plus ultra* of organically evolved and visionary city planning. Even decay is an attraction in itself here: the gnarled or flaking facades somehow add to the beauty of the *palazzi*; the deterioration heightens the mystery. Venice is also the only city in the world where you can still imagine yourself, in almost every place and in whichever direction you look, in 1527, 1679, 1783 or 1856, the precise century being dependent upon whichever *campo* or *salissada* you happen to find yourself in. I stand before paintings dated 1897 and the only things that have evolved on the Campo Manin, the Campo della Salute and on the Scuola Grande are the people, the tall masts of the old sailing vessels and the funnels of steamships. Take a walk with a Baedeker or Murray's travel guide from 1895 and only the prices will have changed. Even if you inspect the skyline from the Campanile on Saint Mark's Square or from the Torre del Bovolo, searching for cracks in the facade of this dream-like city, the illusion remains intact.
§ In any other city you have to root out craftsmanship, mastery, traditions, artisanal pearls... In Venice, they can be found on literally every street. History is tangible here: you can still visit the monastery where Lord Byron translated Armenian manuscripts, you can walk down the street in which Casanova lost his virginity, view the Santa Maria degli Angeli convent where he seduced young novitiates, or admire the Palazzo Vendramin-Calergi and the Palazzo Giustinian in which Richard Wagner composed his beautiful *Tristan and Isolde.* The twenty-first century could not be more remote. Such legitimacy stands in stark contrast to the fake authenticity of the so-called 'Romeo and Juliet House' in Verona, for example. Provided you ignore the street signs designed for lazy tourists and walk away from Saint Mark's Square, it feels as though you are stepping half a century further back in time with every turn of the corner.

Venice is a sensory city. Everything is different here: New Year's Eve, fireworks, snow, the carnival, even sex. Sounds are more intense than anywhere else. Venice is an aural maze: there is no greater pleasure than drinking *un'ombra* on a bridge at dusk and listening to sounds echoing all around, or wandering the streets and being unable to determine whether the noise of the burbling water in the canal is advancing or receding. Venice is almost wholly lacking in anything that could justifiably be deemed a 'nightlife', and yet the atmosphere is often far more decadent than in the post-war cities that position themselves as manic party-centrals. § Many aspects of the city seldom make it into the guidebooks. The largely undiscovered district of Cannaregio. The boat race at the end of May, the Vogalonga, where the trick is to find a spot on one of the terraces that line the Grand Canal. Here, you can watch the flotilla of hundreds of historic and contemporary boats pass by, with the *palazzi* on the opposite bank as a backdrop. The Calle delle Tette, where the courtesans gathered until the beginning of the nineteenth century. The Festa del Redentore, which commemorates the curbing of the plague epidemic in 1575, brings the proceedings to a close with a decadent firework display: also free. Whatever your vantage point, you will reap the rewards of a city that does its utmost to add lustre to every moment, every word and every gesture. § The Venetians are a resourceful people. An ancient but typical example of this trait: in 1573, when the church council rejected Veronese's painting *The Last Supper* on the basis that it contained "too many drunks, dwarves and Germans", the painter, ever the pragmatist, ignored their calls to modify the canvas and took an alternative approach – instead of altering the work he simply revised the title to *The Feast in the House of Levi*. § Far away from the throngs of tourists in San Marco, but still within walking distance, are some of my favourite but lesser-known places. The beautiful Teatro Malibran, which would have been demolished as early as 1835 had it not been saved by the singer Maria Malibran, who sang a benefit performance. Or the various *scuole,* the beautiful buildings that not only provide education but also offer refuge and political support. Attend a chamber music concert in the opulent but never garish halls of the Scuola Grande or the Scuola San Rocco and you will imagine yourself to be the guest of the Doge himself. And even if your grasp of Italian is too shaky to be able to follow the plot, you will never regret attending a play in the Goldoni. The theatre is named after the eighteenth-century playwright Carlo Goldoni who not only authored 130 scripts but also found the time to sire twelve children (or at least: twelve legitimate plus illegitimate triplets). Goldoni was another pragmatist, a man who gave gondoliers free tickets to his premieres because he knew that their recommendations could make all the difference between a success or a flop. Use your wits: visit the Palazzo Ducale as early as possible but do not register for the run-of-the-mill tourist tour. Take the *Itinerari Segreti* instead and discover, in a much smaller group, the most obscure corners of the palace.

Finally, be empathetic towards the locals: imagine what it is like to live in a place where hordes of people stare at your house every day and pollute your city. Venice loves civilised guests, but not boorish invaders.

VINI MERIDIONALI
DENTISTA

VENDITA LIQUORI E
4845
35

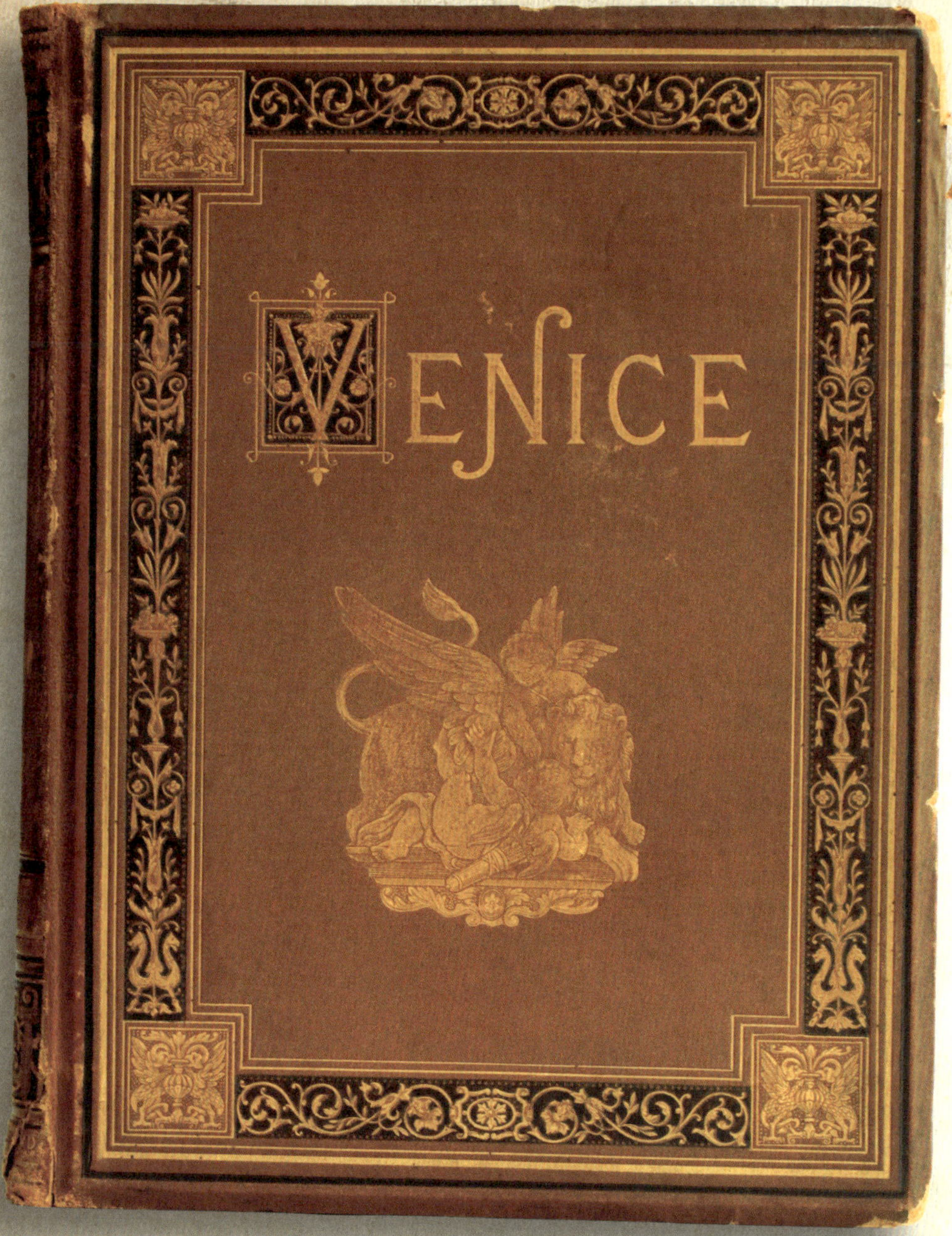
VENICE

VOYAGE
A VENISE

ALBERGHI

This book is emphatically not a travel guide, and I would not waste a chapter on the hotels in any other city, but everything is exceptional about Venice.

Here, all the historic buildings have been preserved, although their functions have often been altered or their original uses have disappeared into **the mists of time.**

More than one residence began life as a ca' or palazzo, only to be converted into a hotel and then back into a private home before finally becoming a museum or government building. It is thrilling to learn about the micro-history of the city from correspondence and hotel guest books, many of which shed light onto some of the blind spots in the official historiography.

DANIELI
WILLKOMMEN
DANIELI

At times, the whole of Venice seems to exude the faded glory of an out-of-season grand hotel. When comparing the historic hotels with the information in a Baedeker or Murray travel guide from 1869 or 1904, often the only things to have drastically changed are the prices. This is not always a good thing – the strict building regulations and the fact that everything in Venice is a protected monument makes it one of the most complicated and expensive cities in the world for hotel renovations. The budget establishments, on the other hand, are anachronisms whose water supply and heating lag far behind the rest of the civilised world. The golden rule when staying in Venice: the simpler the hotel, the more overpowering the stench and noise. But the top hotels are museum-quality mausoleums, cocoons laden with the patina of former illustrious guests – provided you do not stay in a characterless modern annexe such as those at the Bauer or Danieli, of course. § Since anyone who is anyone has visited Venice at some point over the centuries, the city's history is, to a certain extent, also that of Western civilisation. Nearly all the world's most celebrated writers, composers and artists have, at some time or other, resided in Venice's grandiose *alberghi*.

The island of San Clemente was successively a monastery (until abolished by Napoleon), a residence for the Doge's guests, a lunatic asylum and a luxury hotel. We once stayed in a room where electric shock therapy had been administered and to which Mussolini's wife, Ida Dalser, had been 'taken' in 1940 (read: imprisoned). In a letter dated 1850, Effie Ruskin mentions "the mad women of San Clemente" (their male counterparts were quarantined at San Servolo). Her letter also conveys a sense of how thrilling it was for distinguished young ladies to visit the madmen, but always with a chaperone: "Priests here are notoriously scandalous, and San Clemente houses dozens of them, a more hideous collection of crooks you've never seen...".

Behind San Clemente lies the Orfano Canal in which prisoners condemned to death were drowned "in the silence of the night", which is why fishing in those waters was strictly forbidden. § The Palazzo Coccina Tiepolo later became the Papadopoli and, due to the owner's lack of resources, was recently converted into a luxury hotel. To sleep in a room with an illustrious history is a unique experience characteristic of Venice. For ardent readers and obsessive history sleuths like me, it is inspiring to spend the night in Room 202 of the Ca' Sagredo Hotel, for example, which once housed the Count's library. § In order to out-do his father-in-law, he enlarged the windows of the Palazzo Grimani so that they exceeded the scale of the Tiepolo's principal gate, directly opposite. The other Palazzo Tiepolo, owned by the family that spearheaded the failed rebellion of 1310, and the adjoining Palazzo Giustinian, were known as the Hotel Britannia in the nineteenth century, and are today called the Hotel Europa and Hotel Regina. Mary Gaskell, muse of Edward Coley Burne-Jones and other members of the Pre-Raphaelite brotherhood, also stayed at the Hotel Britannia "on the Grand Canal", at that time one of the city's most prestigious addresses. Only when you understand the vagaries of the hotel names can you identify the locations mentioned in the letters of guests such as Proust, Gautier and Verdi, or which crop up in contemporaneous travel writing.

Conversely, numerous of the illustrious eighteenth- and nineteenth-century *grands hôtels* have since closed and been converted back into anonymous palazzi, such as the house that was known as the Pension Suisse in 1878 and was renamed the Hôtel de Rome. Baron Corvo stayed at the now extinct Hôtel Belle Vue et de Russie in Calle Larga San Marco. The house on the Ramo dei Fuseri where Goethe lodged in 1786 temporarily became the Hotel Victoria in 1896, which was helpful for the clients who could not pronounce La Regina d'Inghilterra. "I can now really enjoy the solitude for which I have longed so ardently", Goethe wrote. "Perhaps in Venice there is only one person who knows me, and he will not come in contact with me all at once." § From another letter, I discovered that the eccentric Contessa Marie Wimpffen, who "never leaves her bed", first became a recluse in the Palazzo Fini in around 1850 before moving to the Grand Hotel Palazzo Contarini Fasan which, according to legend, was once home to Shakespeare's Desdemona. The Palazzo Grassi used to be the prestigious hotel known as The Emperor of Austria. According to Harrison Rhodes, the manager of the establishment allowed the Queen of Spain to stay for free, "in exchange for the charisma that her presence afforded". In 1878, Browning lodged in the Palazzo Brandolin-Rota, also known as the Albergo dell'Universo, on the Ponte dell'Accademia. Lord Byron wrote a number of letters from a certain Hotel Gran Bretagna on the Grand Canal, although it is impossible to identify the exact palazzo it occupied. § The red building to the right of Palazzo Corner-Loredan and Ca'Farsetti – an ensemble that now constitutes the Town Hall – was known as the Albergo del Leon Bianco between 1700 and 1880. This is the establishment in which the Emperor Joseph and Catherine the Great stayed, and where William Turner painted the beautiful cityscapes that he observed from his window. As an aside, his room has since been converted into a toilet. It is impossible to recognise such panoramas today because Turner cheated with perspective and adapted the views to the taste of his clients, even going so far as to reposition entire rows of buildings when it suited him. This is also the hotel in which James Fenimore Cooper – then a living legend,

HÔTEL ROYAL DANIELI
HÔTEL ROYAL DANIELI
Venise July 22. 1908.
Dear Grandmother:-
We had such a nice
time at Venice and
left there yesterday for
Milan. This is a
picture of our hotel - it

BAUER GRÜNWALD
GRAND HOTEL D'ITALIE
VENISE
BAUER GRÜNWALD
GRAND'HOTEL
D'ITALIE
NOUVEAU EDIFICE ET TERRASSE DE DEJEUNER
DIRECTEMENT SUR LE GRAND CANAL

now completely forgotten – wrote *The Bravo* in 1831, a novel about spies during the time of the Doges. I am not keen on Cooper because he clearly did not like Venice, as evidenced by a letter dated 1838: "Venice is monotonous and wearying… A town in which the sounds of hoof and wheel are never known, in which the silence of the narrow ravine-like canals is seldom broken… it fatigues by its unceasing calm… I do not recollect ever to have been so tired of a residence in a capital." § Even the Torre del Bovolo, the so-called 'tower of the snail', was once a hotel. In ancient times, the Calle larga dell'Ascensione contained two guest houses for crusaders, the Selvadego and the extant Locanda Luna, the latter of which has been a hotel since the fifteenth century and was once home to the Templars. Certain knights claimed that there were no infidels south of the Luna, but only because they did not bother to venture any further. The building on the far right of the Fondaco dei Tedeschi, which was known as the Sturgeon until the sixteenth century, was also an inn for crusaders, wayfarers and pilgrims – it can be identified in Carpaccio's painting *The Miracle of the Cross at the Ponte di Rialto* from 1494.

The Danieli (founded in 1822 by the hotelier Giuseppe Dal Niel who changed his name to the more sophisticated-sounding Joseph Danieli) occupies the fourteenth-century Palazzo Dandolo and, up until the nineteenth century, was still known as the 'Royal Danieli' or 'Albergo Reale Danieli'. The building is clearly visible in a drawing by Barbari from 1500 – no other hotel in the world can say that it has remained unchanged in all that time. § The first opera was performed in the residence in 1630: *The Rape of Proserpina.* § It is fascinating to see who was considered worthy of mention in which era. In *Venezia,* a German book published in 1894, an entire column is dedicated to the fire-eating Duke of Brunswick's stay at the Danieli. Not a word about Charles Dickens, Richard Wagner, Balzac, Proust and the other great artists who also lodged at the establishment. Names as a measure of the zeitgeist. § This is also the building in which Balzac wrote his romantic novel *Gambara.* Alfred de Musset composed poetry in Room 10 before he fell ill and his mistress, George Sand, embarked on an affair with the treating physician, Doctor Pagello. The Albergo Danieli is mentioned several times in Sand's *Leone Leoni.* § John and Effie Ruskin stayed in Room 32, situated in the left-hand corner of the piano nobile. In *Praeterita*, Ruskin writes: "…the beginning of everything was in seeing the gondola-beak come actually inside the door at Danieli's, when the tide was up the water was two-feet deep at the foot of the stairs." Even the most luxurious hotels offered little in the way of comfort back in 1849: "It was so cold in our hotel that we played Battledore and Shuttlecock in the big hall so as not to freeze". § In 1172, Doge Vitale Michael II was stabbed to death in the alley adjacent to the Danieli and his attackers fled to a nearby house. The Council of Ten razed the property to the ground and decreed that the plot would remain vacant forever... a ruling that was observed until 1948, when, as is all too common nowadays, modern pragmatism prevailed over sacred oaths and the Danieli's ugly annexe arose. Pity the naive tourist who envisages sleeping in a palazzo, pays through the nose for the privilege and wakes up in a soulless modern wing. Nor is the Venetian averse to praising the glorious history as a way of selling the inglorious modernity. § A little further along the Riva degli Schiavoni is the Hotel Metropole where Sigmund Freud, Thomas Mann and Marcel Proust stayed.

The Gritti Palace, which in the nineteenth century was initially called 'Palazzo Swift' and then 'Casa Wetzlar', was also home to John Ruskin in 1851. And for admirers of his work, the author stayed in the corner room on the second floor, facing the side canal. By the nineteenth century, however, all its windows had disappeared behind wooden belvederes. The palazzo once boasted a side entrance, now bricked up, through which gondolas could enter the building and glide up to the reception desk. Since there is no trace of Ruskin in the Gritti, I can only assume that the contemporary management are oblivious to the fact that the aesthete once wrote in the hotel. They prefer, instead, to name-drop the latest Hollywood stars (whose signatures I spotted in the hotel register). Ruskin, ever restless, also stayed in the charming Calcina pension on Zattere, in the Hotel Europa and at Raydon Brown's house. § Ernest Hemingway chatted to the gondoliers from his balcony at the Gritti and used to throw them bottles of wine. § The Palazzo Pisani-Gritti, or at least the central wing, dates back to the fifteenth century. Doge Andrea Gritti lived and died in the building: he suffered a fatal heart attack after partaking of a lavish banquet. The name of the Gritti Palace Hotel is written with a double 't', but my gold coin, minted during the reign of Andrea Grit(t)i, shows it to have once been singular.

The Lido did not begin to be developed until the early nineteenth century. I have heard several connoisseurs of British history proclaim that Lord Byron, exhausted after his dare-devil horseback race, recovered his strength at "his beloved" Hotel Des Bains. But in Byron's day, the Lido was a desolate and somewhat sinister plain, a long, narrow island with wide beaches and which accommodated, as Goethe writes, "the burial-place of Englishmen, and, a little farther on, of the Jews. Both alike are refused the privilege of resting in consecrated ground." When Des Bains was erected in around 1900, Byron had already been dead for eighty years. It was only with the belle époque that the Lido became fashionable as a stylish resort and spa. Byron's macho race against a Prussian officer began at the Church of San Nicolò on the island and ended at the Rialto Bridge. Byron won. § John Ruskin also enjoyed walking and meditating in the area, while his wife Effie's diary tells us that well-educated gentlewomen such as herself would swim at the Lido every day because, even in 1860, the Grand Canal was apparently "...far too dirty. Mrs Brown kindly lent me two old sails with which my gondoliers construct in a few minutes a very serviceable sort of tent where, with Mary's aid, I undress and dress... the beach is deserted, because the Venetians rarely, if ever, swim here. Around five o'clock we sail back to be in time for dinner." § From letters dated 1906, I have discovered that Des Bains initiated the 'Lord Byron Cup', a swimming competition aimed at the mostly British clientele. A motorboat race, under the honourable auspices of the louche Count Giuseppe Volpi di Misurata, was also inaugurated. Noel Coward, who praised Venice as "without doubt the most unique thing the civilised world has to offer", also swam at the Lido. § In more recent times, it was visited by Hemingway who commissioned a portrait bust from the eccentric sculptor Antonio Lucarda, who recounted: "Ernest was impatient, he couldn't sit still, wanted to drink and talk and box while I tried to work. Twice he knocked over the bust and I had to start all over again".

My favourite hotel – the refined, understated and utterly discreet Grand Hotel Des Bains – is a story unto itself. Built in 1900, it was conceived by two Italian architects with impeccable taste, Raffaelo and Francesco Marsich. § Des Bains, thank God, escaped the trend for renovation that saw other hotels sacrifice authentic design elements for the sake of sensible but characterless 'improvements'. The aristocratic grandeur of the Liberty-style marble staircase; the weighty keys with royal blue tassels (as if you are being handed not just the key to your room but to the city itself); the creaking parquet; the linen and silverware; the gated lift with a grille; the dining room decorated with frescoes, boiserie and Venetian chandeliers; the stately landings; the belle époque winter garden, pagoda and patio; the 'secret' tunnel to the beach and the old-fashioned bathing huts: there is no better place in which to read *Death in Venice*, which mentions the hotel by name.

It is not hard to still feel part of the fin de siècle at Des Bains, especially when, as we have seen on several occasions, an Italian wedding reception is held at the hotel and the guests are attired in belle époque gowns and suits. § From the perfectly preserved ballroom – a jewel of bronze, wrought iron and sculpted wood – you can access the upper floor via a hidden spiral staircase in the corner. In 1981, I discovered some plaster fragments that once formed part of the sets for Visconti's *Death in Venice.* Scenes from *The English Patient* were also filmed at Des Bains, with the building standing in for Shepherd's Hotel in Cairo. That atmosphere lingers on: Des Bains could easily be a nexus for spies, exiles and dowagers. § In the heyday of the foxtrot and Charleston it played host to themed parties with titles such as 'Grand Bal Nocturne', 'The Zanzibar Oasis' and 'Tableaux Vivants'.

EXCELSIOR PALACE HOTEL
LIDO-VENEZIA

RICORDO di VENEZIA
CORTILE DEL PALAZZO DUCALE
LA RIVA DEGLI SCHIAVONI
PROPRIETA' RISERVATA
Liebe Marie!

Photographs from the period show femmes fatales posing with greyhounds on the beach. § In *Death in Venice*, which was written in 1911, Thomas Mann described Des Bains as a hotel that continued to employ a liveried bellboy and where the guests still dressed for dinner in their finest evening wear, "that internationally recognised uniform of civilization". A description from the novel that still holds true today reads: "The car was waiting to transport him and other travelers to the Hotel Excelsior from where the motor launch would carry everyone through a private canal to the station." § Mann stayed in Room 214/15 on several occasions, as did many stars of the silver screen, such as Clark Gable and Greta Garbo. We prefer the fourth floor, which is quieter and offers a panoramic view of Venice and the spacious garden below. For no matter how delightful one finds the city, light, air, space and greenery are precious commodities amongst this orgy of stone. § The future of this unique property hangs in the balance: the company that initially planned to convert the iconic Des Bains into fifty-eight luxury apartments for the nouveau riche is now bankrupt (thank God) and this elegant oasis was still boarded up at the time of writing. The abrupt sale of the legendary Des Bains to 'outsiders' has also exposed a structural problem within Venice: in response to a barrage of criticism, the government admitted that it could not afford to purchase Des Bains because the city of the Doges "simply has too many monuments and too few taxpayers". And to think that Gustav von Aschenbach believed his own epoch to be decadent! § *La leggenda continua...?*

The nearby Excelsior, which was founded in 1908 – and is not situated next to the beach but actually on it – was once the most extravagant playground for international party animals. Pablo Picasso, Orson Welles, Ava Gardner and Winston Churchill all frequented the bar. From a distance, the neo-Moorish towers of the Excelsior resemble a Byzantine fortress or a castle from *The Thousand and One Nights*. § During the Roaring Twenties, the 'old money' looked down on the mundane Excelsior as 'vulgar'. The correspondence between Evelyn Waugh and Ann Fleming mentions "the ghastly Excelsior" and "the horrors of speedboats in the lagoon". Waugh preferred the "the melancholy, misty, desolate Venice in January, with not an American in sight." Now considered to be the height of sophistication by film stars, the Cipriani Hotel was once described, for example by Nancy Mitford, as a "vulgar" den for styleless "show-offs". § Des Bains and the Excelsior are certainly expensive but the ritual of travelling to and from Venice in a mahogany Riva yacht – a *motoscafo* – is worth its weight in gold.

Lido - Venezia
2679 - F.lli Garbisa - Venezia.
Grand Hôtel des Bains
Lido Venezia

Hôtel Europa
P. Salviati Venezia

Le Grand-Hôtel

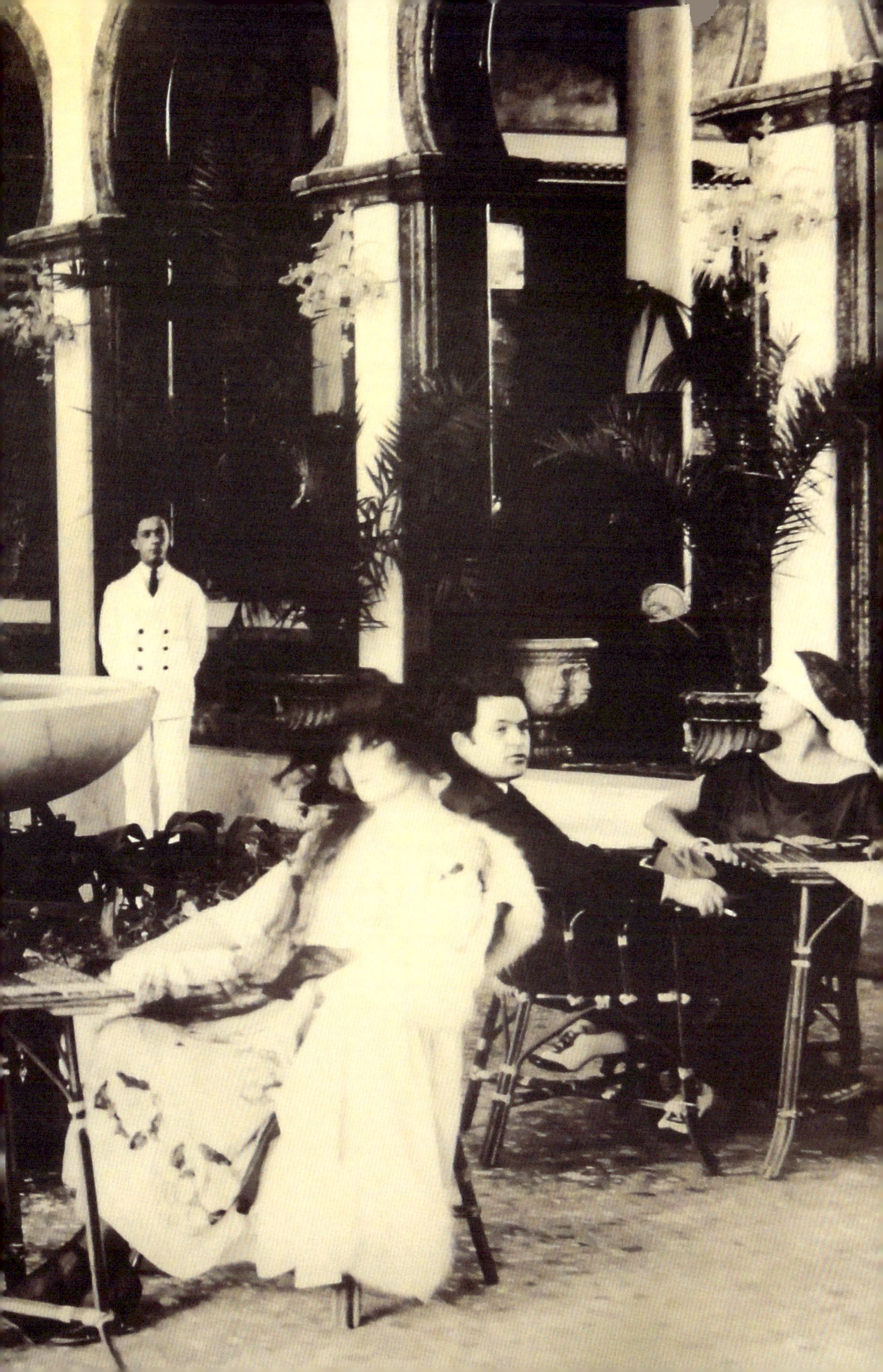

VENEZIA
VÉNISE MONUMENTAL
A. GUÉRINET
Editeur des Musées Nationaux
140, Faubourg Saint-Martin
PARIS
Palais Ducal et Colonne

PATRIMONIO

Venice is perhaps

the only city on the planet

that has not fallen victim to the rapid descent into uniformity.

One of the consequences of globalisation, especially in the West, is that cities are becoming increasingly interchangeable in terms of architecture. They all boast the same retail chains in near-identical shopping centres, similar government buildings and museums, uniform streets and, here and there, a Guggenheim.

SCALA PRINCIPALE

DEL

PALAZZO CONTARINI-DAL-BOVOLO (VENE

RESTAURO

dell'Arch.° Prof. CASTELLAZZI

Cromo Lit. Fior. Firenze

...ANCO di GIUSTIZIA

NEL

...LAZZO PRETORIO

DI

...PISTOIA (TOSCANA)

Da uno Studio

DI

ALFREDO MELANI

Architetto

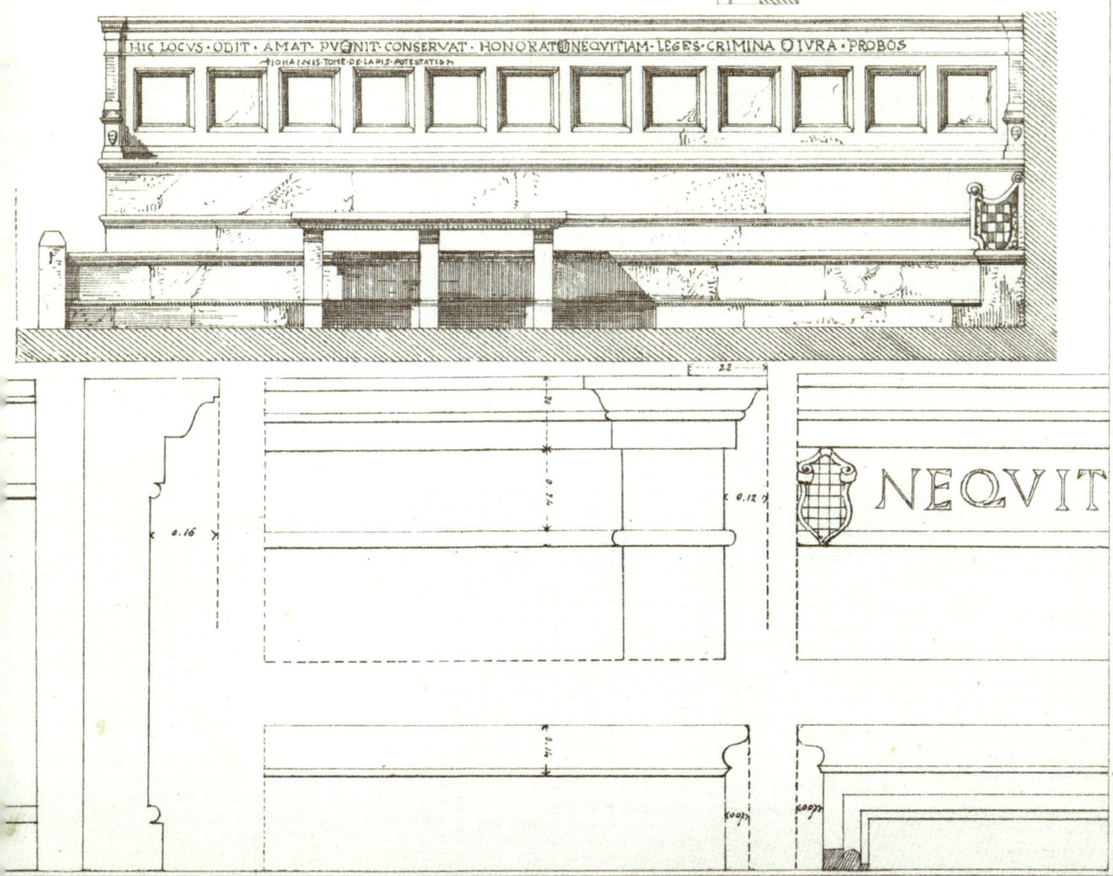

It is ironic, if not cynical, that an architect such as Rem Koolhaas was appointed director of the Venice Biennale in 2014 because, had he and his like-minded colleagues been given free rein in the years between, say, 1945 and now, then roughly half of La Serenissima's pre-war splendour would have been replaced by (post)-modern monstrosities. The consequence of which would have been that Venice, as we know her today, would simply not exist: her uniqueness would have been diluted, her architectural splendour turned into a hotchpotch of egotistical statements rendered in sub-standard materials. § Venice, even more so than Bruges, is perhaps the finest example of the vital need to protect the built heritage. In Venice, the aesthetic ideal has not been undermined, watered down or raped. The charm of the city lies in the fact that she has not been blighted by modern architecture (although souvenir stalls and careless, disrespectful tourists are a hindrance, but that is another story). And this is yet one more reason why people adore visiting the city: on a subconscious level, Venice offers solace. The modern-day tyranny of eternal renewal terrorises us all. In Venice, on the other hand, the beauty of decay reigns supreme. § As it is so beautifully put in English, Venice is 'preserved in its own juice', meaning pure, natural, untainted, intact. This city has reinvented itself, of course: in the fifteenth century "all the gold and power in Christendom flowed through Venice". Today, it is a provincial city that, even within Italy, lacks economic and political clout. Yet Venice is a fine example of passive aggression: the city that has resolutely ignored progress throughout the centuries is finally reaping the rewards of her inflexible stance.

Escalier Mineli

CHIESE E CAMPANE

That Venice is heaven on earth can also be deduced from the number of churches. Here, there are more places of worship per square kilometre than in Malta, and the hundreds of alleyways resound with the clamour of bells. The belfries resemble the masts of ships. A carillon for a Catholic holiday or a wedding can always be heard somewhere, as if there is infinite good news to proclaim. § Not that Venice was always such a religious city. She locked horns with the Pope in Rome on several occasions. And anyone interested in the separation of church and state will find the following detail extremely telling. When Pope Paul V, born Camillo Borghese, ordered the excommunication of Venice in 1606, a rebellious Venetian priest asserted: "I await a sign from the Holy Spirit". To which the Council of Ten replied: "We have already received a sign: that recalcitrant priests should hang." Yet other clerics drank from chalices in which the communion wine was laced with poison. § Long ago, the Venetians knew exactly which bell would chime at which hour. The sound of the *Malefico* (the 'culprit'), the smallest and most ominous of all the bells in the Campanile, pierced the ear drums and brought the Venetians out in goose bumps, for it heralded an execution. When *La Marangone* (or 'carpenter's bell') sounded each morning, the workers knew they had just thirty minutes to reach the Arsenale. § Whenever I am in Venice, I always pay a visit to the city's oldest church: the San Giacometti. Founded in 421 and rebuilt in 1080, the interior and surroundings make you feel as though you have stepped back in time a thousand years. In the tiny square I once saw an extremely elderly pastor of the old school, a Don Camilo-like character, who was watching over a group of young disabled people. He seemed to have drifted away from his principal duties and become something of a social worker, a jack-of-all-trades and the guardian of the district. His true status seemed to have been eroded and undermined and this was all that was left: he was more an unarmed foot soldier than a man of God. § The most bizarre church of all is the SS Giovanni e Paolo, otherwise known as the San Zanipolo. It boasts a masonry wall, which has been plastered and overpainted with... a brick motif. In 1609, William Lithgow described how a monk was executed on the square before the Mendicanti e Ospedaletto (a home for illegitimate children) for having impregnated fifteen nuns in the space of a year. § That Venice boasts so many convents is related to the fact that the Doges were only selected from the ranks of the eldest bachelors in the city, a convention that prevented married fathers from vesting power in their sons and thus cementing a dynasty. As a result, patricians forbade their eldest sons to wed. This led to a lack of suitors and a host of unmarried daughters being placed in convents. Imagine being a young woman within a rich patrician family: growing up ensconced in a cocoon of silk and gold brocade, opulence and abundance as part and parcel of everyday life... only to suddenly find yourself banished to a spartan convent. This created a typically Venetian culture of decadence within their sacred walls as a form of protest. Yet there were many other reasons (or excuses) why women were despatched to convents. When Chiaretta Loredan, the daughter of a famous patrician, fell in love with a poor carpenter who worked at the Arsenale, her father said: "If you insist on marrying a carpenter, then it may as well be Jesus Christ". Being a nun, however, was also a position of standing. Even Tintoretto's daughters, Perina and Alturia, took the veil.

8009.
VENEZIA. CON
AZZA SAN

6735. P. Z. - VENEZIA, PALAZZO VENDRAMIN.

La Piazzetta col Palazzo Ducale e la Riva degli Schiavoni.

1113 P Z. VENEZIA. LA CA D'ORO

5

11

VENEZIA - Rio Contarini

ITALY
K

RICORDO DI VENEZIA
64 VEDUTE

C. NAYA VENEZIA
CAFFE GIARDINO REALE

C. NAYA VENEZIA
105

C.NAYA
VENEZIA
36

C.NAYA
VENEZIA

DENONTIE SECRETE
CONTRO CHI OCCVLTERÃ
GRATIE ET OFFICII.
Õ COLLVDERÃ PER
NASCONDER LA VERA
RENDITA D̃ ESSI

CALLI E PONTI

No other city boasts as many eccentric street names or references to long-lost occupations as Venice: Frezzeria (fletchers), Spadaria (swordsmiths), Calle dei Bombardieri (artillery makers), Calle de la Casselleria (the craftsmen who fashioned bridal chests), Calle dei Pestrin (the milkmen's street), Salissada del Pignater (potters' alley), the Chiesa degli Scalzi (Church of the Discalced [barefoot] Carmelites) and the Calle della Morte (death alley, leading to the site of executions). The Ponte della Paglia is an allusion to straw and dates back to the time when large swathes of Venice were still green and undeveloped, with horses grazing in the fields. § Immigrants are immortalised in names such as Calle delle Turchette (street of the Turkish women), Riva degli Schiavoni (Dalmatians), Campo de Mori (square of the Arab merchants) and Palazzo Mastelli (house of the buckets, because it was said that the Moors owned thousands of pails filled with gold coins). Street names often reference the ubiquitous water: *squero* (shipyard), *rio terrà* or *piscina* (filled-in canal), *molo* (quay) and *fondamenta* (embankment). Certain things are just as remarkable for not having been immortalised. Venice lacks the tradition of venerating individuals: in our part of the world, a landmark such as Ponte Storto (leaning bridge) would have rapidly acquired the name of some politician or general. § The inconsistencies in the spelling of street names and the allocation of house numbers is partly due to the fact that every district has its own dialect and administrative body. And there are times when even the Venetians are stumped: no one has yet been able to tell me how the Sotoportego del Braccio Nudo (street of the naked arm) acquired its name.

Venice might resemble a solid landmass but it is actually a constellation of 124 islands that are linked by hundreds of bridges. Perhaps this is why Venice boasts more bridges than Bruges. The structures spanning the smaller canals were once privately owned and people paid tolls to cross them. When the Ponte dell'Accademia collapsed in 1843 it was very nearly replaced with a tunnel. Initially, an iron replacement bridge was constructed but John Ruskin, who saw it in 1876, proclaimed it horrendous. § The Ponte dei Pugni (of which there are several) acquired its name for being the site of a fight between the rival Castelloni and Nicoletti families from Dorsoduro. Skirmishes frequently took place on bridges and, due to the lack of railings, the winner was immediately apparent: the person who had not fallen into the water. The bridge in San Barnaba still contains two marble imprints of feet that mark the spot where challengers had to stand. Such fights were long tolerated by the Council of Ten due to the endless need for virile, aggressive citizens on the galleys. Moreover, the rivalries between the clans prevented a concerted rebellion against the authorities – divide and rule could easily have been a Venetian tactic and Machiavelli a Venetian. Yet such conflicts were eventually outlawed due to the excessive number of deaths and injuries. § The Ponte delle Tette owes its name to the whores who were granted the right to bare their assets on the bridge – a ruling passed by the Council in the hope that prostitution would discourage homosexuality. § In 1444, the Rialto Bridge collapsed under the weight of the crowds which had gathered to greet the then legendary Marquis of Ferrara. When the construction of the current bridge commenced in 1588, the merchants complained that it would not be ready "until the vaginas catch fire or the male organs grow nails". The nineteenth-century wrought-iron bridges that seem so charming and appropriate nowadays were considered to be gruesome modern aberrations in their day. The iron Ponte dell'Accademia was dismantled in 1846 and replaced by a 'provisional' wooden structure... which is still going strong. 'Crooked' bridges (which can land some two metres away from their starting embankments) have also never been replaced.

ACQUA ALTA

The *acqua alta* makes an already impractical city even more impractical. The city's high tides are completely unrelated to rain or floods and are caused by wind and fluctuations in atmospheric pressure. At times, the water rises by more than a metre and can even peak at two, as recorded in 1966. Some districts are flooded up to sixty times a year. The Piazza San Marco, located in the lowest part of the city, is flooded forty times a year, with the spring tide rising by a metre on around four occasions. At times like this, the doorways of shops and palazzi are boarded up and waves ripple throughout the city, while gangplanks on posts create a criss-crossed obstacle course that is navigated in wellingtons. The red-and-white striped poles are reflected in the water like candy canes and I once saw a fish swimming down the middle of the street. § At *acqua alta*, it becomes impossible to see where the Lagoon ends and the Piazza San Marco begins. The tides are akin to a counterattack by the sea, as though it is striving to reclaim the land that it has lost to the Venetians. When a spring tide reaches a height of 122 centimetres, some 32% of the city is flooded. At 140 centimetres, half of Venice is affected.

While a state of emergency would be declared in any other city, this is regarded as a perfectly normal situation in Venice. § One could even say that La Serenissima has always been flooded, although the Lagoon reneges on its unspoken agreement at *acqua alta*. The most magical moment of all is when the waters begin to rise, but not just, or not only, from the Lagoon: they often bubble up from between the stones on a square, as if thousands of fountains of sparkling water have suddenly been switched on beneath your feet. I know people who only come to Venice between October and March in the hope of experiencing the *acqua alta* – a form of aesthetic disaster tourism that is not appreciated by the Venetians. § A council of wise men was appointed to consider the *acqua alta* as early as 1500. The course of the River Brento was diverted to save Venice and the Lagoon. If you count the submerged steps of a palazzo, you can see that the water level is now 50 centimetres higher than it was in the seventeenth century. At the Ca' da Mosto, the goods entrance was situated relatively high above the water level to ensure that deliveries of herbs or silk robes remained dry. You will also notice algae stains up to a metre above the pavement on certain facades; and up to eight metres above the water level one can also observe the damage caused by salt, with such marks distinguishing

LA DOMENICA DEL CORRIERE

Supplemento settimanale illustrato del nuovo CORRIERE DELLA SERA - Abbonamenti: Italia, anno L. 1165, sem. L. 625 - Estero, anno L. 1765, sem. L. 925

Anno 52 — N. 52 24 Dicembre 1950 L. 25,—

L'"acqua alta„ a Venezia. L'aumento del livello della Laguna ha fatto nuovamente allagare piazza San Marco dove si son dovute installare alcune passerelle volanti. Ma dove non c'erano passerelle, volonterosi portatori provvedevano a traghettare sulle spalle i passanti più frettolosi. (Dis. di G. De Gaspari)

Venice's palazzi from those on the Italian lakes where the water is fresh. Some three hundred years ago, Casanova would have known a much higher and less water-filled Venice, with taller steps. Since then, the sloping floors of the Basilica, which are said to mimic the rise and fall of the waves, have simply been warped by the moisture and affected by the salt. Without flood defences, the crypt – originally built above the water level – would be inundated at every high tide.

Venice is a sublime aberration: a stone city built on wooden piles sunk into the water. When a 50-metre stretch of canal was exposed in Cannaregio, I could clearly see how rotten the foundations of the palazzi were, how the stones were not only damp but porous and crumbling, a mass of gaping holes beneath the water. I also noticed that the canal was far shallower than I had imagined: 1.5 metres at the deepest point and 0.5 metres at the shallowest. I also spied a stone pipe that had not seen the light of day since 1750. The foundations of palazzi rest on wooden piles that have been driven into the mire. Provided they are not exposed to the open air, they do not rot but petrify or fossilise. As early as 1855, Robert Browning refrained from buying the Palazzo Montecuccoli because of "the shaky foundations". § An additional drawback being that the wood in palazzi will warp and the walls crack, simply because such immense houses do not sink uniformly. Stand directly in front of the Ca' da Mosto and you will immediately notice that the subsidence is greater to the right. Having visited several privately owned palazzi as a guest, I have seen the signs that testify to the constant battle against the damp: wet patches on the walls, but also books that have turned to pulp, split parquet floors, cracks in the plaster... The beautiful Istrian stone used in Venice is not an aesthetic choice: it is non-porous and functions as a water barrier. The same is true of trachyte, the volcanic stone with which the streets are paved. § Once, when I was staying at the Danieli, the *acqua alta* got the better of me – the hotel became the most beautiful prison in the world for a period of twenty hours. In 1867, John Ruskin described how the gondolas glided into the Danieli's lobby on the spring tide, at a time when the first three steps of the imposing marble staircase were completely submerged. On another occasion, while seated on the Cipriani's terrace, we experienced one of the flash storms that are so typical of the region: from beautiful June weather and temperatures of 32 degrees to a hailstorm in under four minutes. § But Venice triumphs over all other cities in this regard: good weather is not a must since it is just as pleasurable to wander through misty, rainy and flooded streets. I have always regretted not having been in Venice in 1929: that was the year in which the city froze and you could walk across the ice from the Piazza San Marco to Torcello. §

CAFFÈ FLORIAN

Other than in Venice, where else can you drink, philosophise and dine in elegant eighteenth-century cafés? I will be eternally grateful to Floreano Francesconi for his inspired idea to establish a *bottega da caffè* in 1720. This opportunistic patriot christened his coffee house Alla Venezia Trionfante, although it soon became known by its nickname, Florian. What you do not read in the contemporary publicity for the Florian is that a brothel operated on the top floor of the *caffè* until the mid-nineteenth century. Officially, it was a *bagnio,* or Turkish bath, although the term was typically used as a euphemism for a house of ill repute. § Coincidentally, it was also in the Florian, beginning in 1760, that the first newspaper was distributed, the *Gazzetta Veneta,* which was named after the small coin that was handed over in payment for each edition. The word 'gazette' is thus of Venetian origin. § During this period, the Florian also boasted first-floor balconies, which were occupied by the nobility during festivities as though boxes at the opera.

One of the most pleasing aspects of Venice is that you can literally run your fingertips along walls, facades, tables and partitions that have been touched by legendary figures – the last serious renovation dates back to 1858. The patina of the walls suggests that all the conversations here have been covered with a layer of varnish by the greats. In this orgy of marble, gold leaf, mahogany and blood-red velvet, a chamber opera is performed on a daily basis. § Too many hotels and restaurants brag, often fraudulently, about their illustrious and historical customers. But here it has been conclusively proven that Casanova, Oscar Wilde, Jean-Jacques Rousseau, Montesquieu, Chateaubriand, Lord Byron, Percy Bysshe Shelley, George Sand and Alfred de Musset, Alexandre Dumas, Napoleon Bonaparte, Johann Wolfgang von Goethe, Madame de Staël, Charles Dickens, Frederick Rolfe (alias Baron Corvo), Thomas Mann, Henry James, Richard Strauss and Marcel Proust all spent time in the same elegant *séparés* and *salotti* (salons) that can still be enjoyed today. As did, at a later date, Evelyn Waugh (the Florian is mentioned in his masterpiece *Brideshead Revisited*), Graham Greene, Orson Welles, Maria Callas, Placido Domingo, David Bowie, Astrid Verbeeck and a whole procession of princesses and kings. Balzac described the Florian as a "a stock exchange, a theatre foyer, a reading room, a social club, a confession box". § Richard Wagner and Franz Liszt often frequented the establishment, although they actually preferred the Caffè Lavena.

The proprietors of the Quadri, directly opposite, maintain the traditional standards: their upper floor still houses the most exquisitely decorated restaurant. The Quadri was the first *caffè* in Western Europe to serve genuine Turkish coffee, as of 1775, which for several decades afterwards enjoyed a reputation for "causing debauchery in women when used excessively". Certain figures (perhaps they were tea merchants?) even believed that drinking coffee led to sodomy. The Quadri had a terrible reputation for a good many years and only acquired a more elegant clientele in around 1830. During *acqua alta*, the side of the Piazza San Marco on which it is situated is the first to be submerged. It was also the favourite café of Stendhal, Byron and Dumas.

Florian

The Venetian poet Pietro Buratti wrote the following lines in 1819:

'El gran turco xe da Quadri
Là desusso nei bigliardi
Questo è il logo ove sti ladri
Se riduse co xe tardi'

(After dark, the Quadri is the place where thieves and muggers gather to conspire).

The Piazza San Marco once boasted a great many more cafés, although these have long since disappeared. There were thirty-four in 1759: Regina d'Hungaria, L'Orfeo, Speranza, Fortuna, L'Imperatore, etc. § In 1776, the Council of Ten issued a decree banning women from entering such establishments, and while the ruling was directed at courtesans, the *donne oneste* also suffered. The Caffè Quadri was shunned by Venetians for much of the nineteenth century as it was where the Austrian occupiers and spies congregated. Every café had its own clientele, as I discovered in the Baedeker Travel Guide of 1832: Caffè Suttil ("aristocracy"), Caffè Orientale ("traders and sailors"), Costanza ("Turks and Albanians"), All'Arabo ("Arabs") and Aurora ("all and sundry"). § James Fenimore Cooper mentions, in around 1840, a coffee house that was reserved for "Turks and Muslims". The Caffè Français at No. 110 on the Quadri side, where John Ruskin once stayed and his wife Effie was robbed of her jewels, has also disappeared. In around 1850, the Re di Francia offered "the best restaurant in Venice and elegant rooms". Next door, at No. 109, there used to be a Hotel San Marco.

Today, three orchestras of varying quality perform in the cafés on a rotating basis, whereas in the nineteenth century there was a single ensemble of sixty musicians. Terraces were non-existent: coffee was only consumed under the arcades. § Those who grumble about the prices in the Florian or Quadri seem to forget that immaculate waiters serve exquisite refreshments within miniature museums, and that there is no charge for the orchestra or view of the most beautiful square in the world... and the hot chocolate is second to none. It was once known as *brodo indiano* (Indian brew) in Venice and was often drunk in the morning or as a stimulant before lovemaking. § *Andemo da Florian!*

tempo di Casanova

CARNEVALE

Carnevale.
From *carne* (meat)
and *levare* (to take away),
the giving up of meat after
Mardi Gras – Shrove Tuesday.

In this context, carnival is the last day of feasting before Lent. There is no better place for a carnival than Venice, if only because it seems as though the city has spared no expense or effort when it comes to its own costume. No matter how extravagant the disguises, the city itself will always steal the show. Nowhere else in the world does a single event veer so dramatically between art and kitsch.

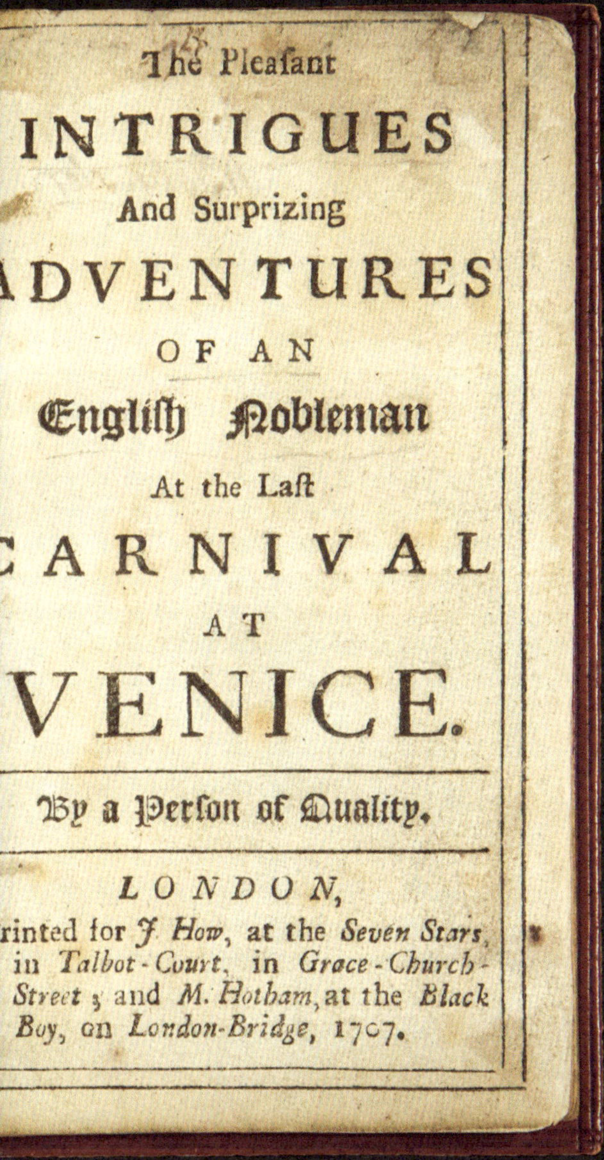

The Pleasant
INTRIGUES
And Surprizing
ADVENTURES
OF AN
English Nobleman
At the Last
CARNIVAL
AT
VENICE.

By a Person of Quality.

LONDON,
rinted for *J. How*, at the *Seven Stars*,
in *Talbot-Court*, in *Grace-Church-*
Street; and *M. Hotham*, at the *Black*
Boy, on *London-Bridge*, 1707.

is a ſtrong Stone Built, Dark Fabr
Beautify'd, within, with extrao
nary fine Painting, and Pav'd w
Stones of more than ordinary
lue ; Adorn'd, without, with cur
Carv'd Figures in Stone ; and o
the great Door are four Ho
Caſt in Braſs, never to be equa
joyning to it is the *Doge*'s ſpac
Palace, and Courts of *Judicat*
which make the fourth part of
Square. At ſome diſtance is
Mark's Steeple, four ſquare , B
with Brick, higher than the *M*
ment on *Fiſh-ſtreet-hill* in *Lon*
and a Noble *Key*, from whenc
beheld the *Adriatick-Sea* ; (at
bottom of which the City is B
on ſeventy odd Iſlands, join'd
eight hundred Stone Bridges)
ſeveral little Neighbouring Iſ
and the main Continent above
Miles off. In this large Squ
People, in Maſquerade, Talk
Intrigue as their Humours ſerve

Almoſt every one is ſo diguiſed n Habit, that there is no knowng any by their Dreſs, when they ppear in the *Piazza*, or at the *Redotto*, a large Publick Building, livided into ſevery Rooms, where s *Gaming*, choice of *Sweet-meats*, *Vines*, all ſorts of *Fruits*, and variety of Entertainment, and a free Converſation with any one: Every Night is ſpent at *Comedies*, *Opera's*, or at ſome Noble *Venetians* Houſe, who gives a *Ball*. By this you nay imagine the *Carnival* to be a onfuſed Scene of intermixt Pleaſure, jumbled together without any Regularity.

Ano: 1710

Once upon a time, the Venetian carnival lasted five months: after centuries of fighting, the city of the Doges could finally relax and the citizens jubilantly took the reins – and thus the orgasmic *dolce far decadentia* was inaugurated. Venetians were allowed to stroll in public, masked, from October until Lent, except during the Christmas Novena. The festivities came to an abrupt halt when the bells of San Marco rang out on Ash Wednesday. § It is interesting to note the epochs in which the carnival was banned or suspended. During the festivities Venice went completely off the rails and turned into a cross between Sodom, Gomorrah and the Baghdad of *One Thousand and One Nights*. A host of new rules and directives reveals, however, a steady increase in abuses. In the fourteenth century, it was forbidden to wear masks when gambling. In 1775, no one was allowed to disguise themselves as a bishop or cardinal. From 1800, "noble ladies were no longer allowed to mingle with courtesans". To discourage misconduct ("blasphemy", "intrigue", "devilish unchastity"), it was forbidden by decree to enter churches or monasteries when in costume or wearing a mask. A wall was even built to prevent the nuns of the convent of San Lorenzo from joining the festivities, although the sisters forced the gate in protest. § In 1797, fearing the presence of spies, the carnival was abolished by Napoleon, and in 1930, Harrison Rhodes wrote that "masked balls are now forbidden". It was not until 1970 that the carnival once again became an uninterrupted annual event.

The wearer of a *bauta* (white mask), *pelerine* (lace collar) and a *tabarro* (cape) was not only concealing their identity but also their social background, thus eradicating all notions of rank and status. In theory! In practice, of course, it was obvious that those who donned extravagant hand-made masks embellished with gold leaf and precious stones were unlikely to be destitute. Certain stereotypical disguises were immensely popular: Pantalone (the avaricious merchant), Dottore or Medico della Peste (the sinister plague doctor wearing a beak-like nose case into which herbs were stuffed), Capitano (a parody of a macho Spanish captain), Brighella (a drunken villain), Arlecchino (the harlequin from the Commedia dell'arte) and, for the women, Pulcinella, Colombina and the professional flirt, Civetta. § During the carnival, Venetians present a unique face to the world: that of anonymous exhibitionists. Anyone who splashes out on a lavish costume and parades through the city for ten days is a show-off and poseur, thus an exhibitionist, but masks guarantee complete anonymity. § In a city where they were de rigueur, eye contact was everything. The choice of make-up also contained subtle codes, such as the numerous types of beauty spots: the *appassionata* at the corner of the eye, the *coquette* above the lip, the *galante* on the chin, and the *assassina* next to the corner of the mouth.

One can still find traces of the ancient carnival here and there, such as in the Calle del Ridotto: this was once the site of the Sala del Ridotto in which the most legendary and decadent balls were held. § That the mask makers – the *mascherari* – were held in high esteem can be deduced from the fact that they were immortalised as statues, which was not the case for other professions.

Thanks to the diaries of socialites from bygone days one can conclude that the carnival was more than just a party. § From an anonymous diary written in 1758: "The bridges are packed with jesters, fire-eaters, acrobats, soothsayers and human pyramids. Boxing matches or bullfights are held on every square. Live dogs are fired like cannonballs. During the running of the bulls through the streets, the bulls are attacked by trained dogs. During the Volo del Turco, an acrobat flew up to the Doge's lodge to offer him a bouquet of flowers. But most spectacular of all was the balloon ride. Just picked up two peasant girls in the *casini*." § Effie Ruskin writes in 1867: "San Marco turned black with the masked people. We watched from a safe distance, the balcony of the palace. Sixty dancers in black and red tried to perform a choreography, but they were swamped and pushed by the crowd. Sweets were thrown, but also glasses of liquor. When dusk fell, the *canaille* took advantage of the situation to surreptitiously touch women. On the way home, in a narrow alley, I asked a masked woman in a Moorish costume for sweets. She opened her Handkerchief and politely said, '*Resta servita, signora*' [Be served, my lady]. I saw a man with a powdered wig and a black mask gazing piercingly in my direction. The masks enter the boxes and do anything they like. But that evening, at the Cavalchina, the most prestigious masked ball at the Opera, I noticed that the local nobility wore powdered wigs and rococo dresses but no masks. I sat next to Princess Hohenlohe. The Duchesse de Berry was also in attendance, still in mourning and without a mask. The rules among the nobility are stricter than I thought: no one is allowed to touch a masked person or walk alongside them without permission. Since the Austrian conflict and under (the republic of) Manin, masks are forbidden because they facilitate spying." § Between 1925 and 1955 the Mitford sisters were often guests of Count Brandolino D'Adda. For them, the Venetian carnival was part of 'the season' which included horse racing at Ascot, visits to Monaco, and sailing and lounging on the French Riviera. Venice was their hide-away: a remote backwater that was hidden from the already prying eyes of the popular press, a provincial town where you could roam freely with your lover. § Deborah Mitford, disguised as the eighteenth-century Duchess Georgiana Spencer, attended Charles de Beistegui's legendary ball at Palazzo Labia in the company of the photographic model Daisy Fellowes. The ball was "an unforgettable theatrical performance with entrées of men and women in exquisite costumes." The empress of Russia attended with "at least three lovers". Guests disguised themselves as "Marie-Antoinette, Farinelli, Don Juan, Madame de Pompadour, Louis XIV, Byron, Casanova, Mozart, pirates, courtesans...". There were "heralds, trumpeters, fire-eaters, living statues, liveried waiters, Pulcinellas clamouring for the guests, courtesans hired for the gentlemen..." not to mention an archdeacon "dressed as a seventeenth-century wench." § Countess Linnea Linderoth writes in 1929: "In the palazzo of Marchesa V., I saw a naked pianist covered in gold paint and leopards who were dosed with morphine before being released among the guests. Elderly Count Targhetta d'Audiffret is said to wear eighteenth-century costume all year round. He is the owner of the Palazzo Merati, where the mother and two sisters of Casanova once lived." Harrison Rhodes also describes how "an aristocratic lady ferried a real leopard around in her gondola." § Actor Peter Ustinov once told me that a Hollywood film director forced him to wear a fake beard because his real one "didn't look real enough". Perhaps that was also the absurd reasoning behind the decision to make the film *Il carnevale di Venezia* entirely in Cinecittà rather than Venice. It strikes me that the choice can be put down to a mixture of stinginess coupled with a sense of amnesia, self-delusion and pride – as if a set could be more real than this unique city.

Only when you have experienced the Venice carnival at its pinnacle, at private balls in palazzi away from the lowbrow tourists with their plastic made-in-China masks (Marco Polo would instantly know!), do you realise how liberating it is to wander around in a mask and costume, although the pleasure must have been even greater in times past, simply because cameras had yet to be invented – and this illusion is preserved at the *Ballo del Doge* in the fifteenth-century Palazzo Pisani Moretta (until someone takes a picture with a flash, that is). It is no coincidence, even an open secret, that numerous celebrities visit Venice to be able to walk around unrecognised for once, albeit masked. One will cross paths with a masked and costumed apparition only to think a few seconds later: hey, I know those eyes and that voice from all those movies. § The best balls are held in the Palazzo Pisani Moretta, the Palazzo Tiepolo, the Palazzo Dandolo (known from 1638 as the Ridotto di San Moisé) and the Ca' Zenobio. By candlelight – the owner once had thirty servants, two of whom did nothing but light and extinguish candles. Anyone who fails to dress up for such an event feels like an unmasked voyeur; and since the carnival is like an improvised play, the Piazza presents its own spectacle. § Sometimes in foggy weather during the carnival you will unexpectedly encounter a handful of costumed revellers in a backstreet. At moments like this, the illusion is complete and you truly imagine yourself to be in 1786. The carnival even comes calling at La Fenice, especially when the orchestra is tuning up and all you can see in the semi-darkness, just before the lights are dimmed, are sparkling jewels and glittering eyes behind a sea of masks. Venetians from, say, 1621, could scarcely have imagined that four hundred years later, crazy modern people would go around pretending to be Doges. But if reincarnation exists, then the law of probabilities dictates that at least some of the costumed tourists will actually be re-enacting their previous lives: be it Doge, patrician, *chevalier* or merchant of Venice… §

AMORE

"Venexia...
no ghê a sto mondo no cità
piu bela par far l'amor."

"You cannot imagine a more beautiful city
in which to make love", wrote
RICCARDO SELVATICO
in the Venetian dialect.

But Mary Lutyens warned:
"Never go to Venice if you're
unhappy." Is that true?

To be single amidst all the sensual,
rhapsodising lovebirds, the bastard
children of Pietro Aretino,
the betrothed and the married is
unbearable – so close to the ardour
and yet having to sleep alone?

In this clinical world where postmodern cool and ironic detachment reign supreme, romantics are an endangered species and, furthermore, we have been conditioned to believe that Venice is a romantic cliché, and thus suspect and to be avoided. But every cliché is based on a primal truth, and Venice is unashamedly romantic. Not to mention infectious: "A realist, in Venice, would become a romantic", as Arthur Symons once observed. § Venice is a city in which everything seems more charged, profound and poetic. Lovers and seducers hope that the magic of Venice will shine upon them. Nowhere else will you find as many lingerie shops. Nor as many jewellers. For lovers, the city is a natural ally: love is of a higher order in Venice because the personal merges with the monumental. And those who are alone or wounded will find comfort here, as did Laurie Lee, who "fled from love into a melancholy city cloaked in November mists, with signs at canal corners saying Andante and Grave". For every honeymooner there is a lonely soul who hopes that Venice will heal a broken heart or help them forget. For both, La Serenissima is the refuge of the last chance.

Out of season and away from the Rialto, the city is completely silent. In all tranquil places, and for Venice this is doubly true, you become better attuned to your inner voice, and therefore also to the whispers of your mind. Without static interference on your mental wavelength your heart's and soul's desires become crystal clear. § Venice has long been a backdrop to amorous intrigues. Casinos were not originally gambling temples but boudoirs, houses of assignation and love nests where paramours, adulterous or otherwise, could hold discreet rendezvous. During the Renaissance Venice boasted over a hundred casinos. § More than any other Italian city, Venice prides herself on the passion she both exudes and inspires. There is no more typical tale than that of Donna Honeste: born in Ca' Cent'anni, in the parish of San Tommaso, she was the wife of a swordsmith. Marchetto Rizzo, a nobleman, fell in love with her. In order to make contact, he ordered a dagger from her husband. But she did not succumb to his advances, so he raped her. Out of shame, she committed suicide... with the aforementioned blade. There appears to be a moral to this story: beware of aristocrats, smiths, thwarted passions and heated emotions. Yet the voice of the Venetian who relayed the account was also inflected with pride and ardour, even intimating that it was a gauche mistake. § While the Venetians were familiar with arranged marriages, patrician families also had the right of veto over wedding contracts through a principal known as *contraddizione*. The architect of San Nicolò dei Mendicoli even provided different exits for two extremely volatile rival clans: when there was a mixed marriage or the baptism of a child from such a union, the Castelloni left the church by the eastern door and the Nicoletti by the southern gate. It says something about the intensity of derailed passions and territorial ambitions when an architect must take such circumstances into account when designing a church. § Girls promised in marriage traditionally presented their dowries at the Santa Maria Formosa church. In 1490, pirates invaded the building and stole both the riches and the brides-to-be. The parish carpenters made chase and recovered the young women – who had already been robbed of their virginity. For centuries, the Doge paid an annual visit to the church in remembrance of this dark episode. § "*Auguri!*" is a cry that you hear daily in Venice, mostly in and around the Santa Maria dei Miracoli. Built in 1489, this is the church where Venetians like to get married. Venice has been lovingly built and renovated. The authenticity of this noble city speaks to newlyweds – other than cheap souvenirs, there is little plastic to be found, and who would not want to forge their own lasting bond in a city of marble, sandstone and gold? There is also plenty of space: Venice seems to have erected a church for every inhabitant, which is what you also find in Malta. With a dash of initiative and a sense of adventure, you will discover silk at affordable prices, or invitations and business cards that are still crafted by hand and printed on an eighteenth-century press. Clever wedding guests book the *altana* in a little hotel, the upstairs room, which usually has a roof terrace. And after the nuptials, where else can you attend a classical concert of Venetian chamber music in one of the authentic palazzi that are opened to the public by impoverished *contesse*? § Every day, foreign couples get married to one another, but also to Venice. In this, they are following in the footsteps of the Doge who used to cast a ceremonial ring into the water every year, thereby symbolically marrying La Serenissima to the sea. The Republic existed for half a millennium. Which means that there are five hundred gold rings nestling in the mud of the Lagoon for patient and persistent treasure hunters... § We often saw weddings at the Hotel Des Bains, for which the guests occasionally dressed up in the style of the belle époque – like a mirage from a bygone age. But we also know of aristocratic Venetians, such as Nani Bernardo, who will fund the exorbitant upkeep of their sinking or subsiding palazzo by vacating the piano nobile and renting it out as a wedding venue (while they themselves live on the second floor). For couples who said 'I do' to each other in Venice and subsequently spent their wedding night in a Venetian bed, is the divorce rate lower than for the lovers who married elsewhere? § A thousand times more children have been conceived in Venice than actually born on its soil, which perhaps explains why the population is declining year on year. But whoever was conceived in the city is also a Venetian.

MÉMOIRES

DE

J. CASANOVA

DE SEINGALT

ÉCRITS PAR LUI-MÊME

SUIVIS DE

FRAGMENTS DES MÉMOIRES DU PRINCE DE LIGNE

Nequidquam sapit qui sibi non sapit..
CIC. AD TREB.

NOUVELLE ÉDITION

COLLATIONNÉE SUR L'ÉDITION ORIGINALE DE LEIPSICK

et ornée de gravures sur bois d'après les dessins

DE MAILLART

Premier grand prix de Rome

TOME CINQUIÈME

PARIS
LIBRAIRIE GARNIER FRÈRES
6, RUE DES SAINTS-PÈRES, 6

Altera nunc rerum facies, me quero; nec adsum
Non sum qui fueram non putor esse: fui.

JACQUES CASANOVA DE SEINGALT
à l'âge de 63 ans

GEORGE LORD BYRON

Venice is a sacred place that we know from the works of Shakespeare and Otway," wrote Lord Byron to his publisher in 1816. "I have not yet sinned here in verse." What he meant was: I am not yet arrogant enough to have attempted to capture the elusive mystery of Venice in poetry. He certainly did not mean to say that he had not yet sinned in the city. § The Palazzo Mocenigo is a constellation of three buildings. Many people mistakenly gaze with fascination at the wrong edifice: between 1818 and 1820, Byron first rented the middle palazzo and later the left, closest to the Rialto. He maintained a retinue of fourteen servants, two gondoliers and thirty pets. § In 1999, I attended a private recital by Cecilia Bartoli at the Palazzo Mocenigo, which was then owned by a mysterious Russian businessman. Accompanied by lute, theorbo and baroque guitar, Bartoli sang eight arias by Vivaldi and Caccini before an audience of thirty people. At one point, I heard a rustling sound behind me. I turned around, annoyed, but it turned out to be Cecilia's mother – and if anyone is allowed to fiddle with their programme then it is the woman who worked hard for nine months to bring this divine voice into the terrestrial world. § The aura of Lord Byron was still palpable in the attic, stairwell and water vestibule where the private gondolas were once moored. I walked across the marble mosaic floor upon which he had once stepped, my fingertips brushing the bronze banister that he clasped for support... Rarely do you come this close to living history because anywhere that was home to a hero some two centuries ago will have long since been renovated into something sterile and unrecognisable. The water vestibule has never been restored, and the floor, wall coverings, lanterns and wall-mounted seats in stone and wood are the eighteenth-century originals. Byron's menagerie used to roam free here: peacocks, monkeys, dogs, a bear, a fox, a wolf and a leopard. § In the Palazzo Mocenigo's garden, I saw the three-metre-high, ostentatious, unfinished statue of Napoleon: a Corsican head upon a muscular, naked Greek super body, an olive branch in one hand and an eagle at his feet. An as-yet uncarved chunk of rough marble between hand and head served as a 'handle' by which to move the statue. The work was intended for the Piazza San Marco, but fate intervened and Napoleon was overthrown before its completion. § The philosopher Giordano Bruno, who was initially hired by the Mocenigo family as a tutor and advisor, was also once a guest at the palazzo, but they eventually reported him to the Inquisition and he was burned at the stake.

Byron lived in Venice for years. He had initially wanted to lodge at the Gritti Palace but it had been reserved months in advance. In his own words: "I like the gloomy gaiety of their gondolas – and the silence of their canals – I do not even dislike the evident decay of the city." These were his most turbulent and productive years, and it was in Venice that he wrote parts of *Manfred*, *Childe Harold* and *Don Juan*. He studied the Venetian dialect and shunned his English compatriots ("I do what I can for them – if they are sick... but little more."). It is even said that he coined the now ubiquitous term 'Bridge of Sighs'. Venice was a natural ally, for Byron loved women, history, mystery, decadence and water. His servant always stashed dry clothes in the gondola in case the master fancied a spontaneous swim. Eye-witness accounts confirm that Byron, wearing full evening dress, once sprang from a window at the Palazzo Albrisi and swam home through the Grand Canal. At night, he carried a torch to avoid being ambushed. He also engaged in a swimming contest with the Cavaliere Angelo Mengaldo, an officer in Napoleon's army who boasted that he was the best swimmer in his regiment. Between four in the afternoon and eight o'clock in the evening, they swam from the Lido to the end of the Grand Canal, almost four kilometres away. Byron would subsequently also brag that he was fatigued that day from "having had a *piece* [sex] in the forenoon – and taking another in the evening at ten of the clock". Harrison Rhodes writes that the 'Lord Byron Gala', a swimming competition in his honour, was held annually until 1930. § All the Venetians were thrilled by the presence of the illustrious poet, society figure, adventurer and freedom fighter... except the men. "I have got some extremely good apartments in the house of a 'Merchant of Venice', who has a daughter in her twenty-second year. Marianna is in her appearance altogether like an antelope. She has the large, black, oriental eyes... then she has the voice of a lute... But her great merit is finding out mine," wrote Byron on 17 November 1816. She was the first of many conquests. Margarita Cogni, alias La Fornarina (the 'little oven'), would follow, whom he described as being "wild as a witch – and fierce as a demon" and as having "the strength of an Amazon with the temper of Medea. She was a fine animal – but quite untameable." § Byron enjoyed riding at the Lido. I know the place well, and it always reminds me of the following incident, which Byron described thus: "In an autumn storm, one day, I went to the Lido to ride horse and go up to Malamocco (the stretch of sand between the Excelsior and the Des Bains, although the hotels were built almost a century later) and back. On our return, I found Margarita on the open steps of the Mocenigo palace, with her great black eyes flashing through her tears, and the long dark hair, which was streaming, drenched with rain, over her brows and breast. The lightning flashing round her made her look like Medea alighted from her chariot, or the Sibyl of the tempest. On seeing me safe, she called out to me.—'*Ah! can' della Madonna, xe esto il tempo per andar' al' Lido*?' (Ah! dog of the Virgin, is this a time to go to the Lido?)." On another occasion, he recounts: "At last she quarrelled with her husband, and one evening ran away to my house. Her husband then applied to the police. She was obliged to return with the poor man, who had a phthisic [tuberculosis]." He went on to describe their break-up: "I was firm, and she went threatening knives and revenge. The next day, she walked in (having broken open a glass door that led from the hall below to the staircase), and advancing straight up to the table, snatched the knife from my hand, cutting me slightly in the thumb in the operation." § Byron also seduced Arpalice Taruscelli... and Countess Guiccioli... and the married Signora Marianna Segati, with whom he had sex at the Cavalchina, the carnival ball (after which the aforementioned gentle tigress "snatched off the mask of Madame Contarini, for no other reason but because she happened to be leaning on my arm"). Byron also went on to have an encounter with Marianna's sister-in-law, as described in a letter from December 1816: "the door of my apartment opened, and in walked a well-looking girl of about nineteen, who informed me that she was married to the brother of my *amorosa*, and wished to have some conversation with me. I made a decent reply... when, to my very great astonishment, Marianna S *, without a single word seizes her said sister-in-law by the hair, and bestows upon her some sixteen slaps. You need not be alarmed – duels on love matters are unknown – at least, with the husbands."

§ Percy Bysshe Shelley, however, wrote: “Venetian women are perhaps the most contemptible of all who exist under the moon; they smell so of garlick that an ordinary Englishman cannot approach them.” Adding of Byron “he says he dissaproves, but he endures.” Shelley and his muse, Mary Godwin, arrived in Venice with Byron’s former mistress, Clare Clairmont. She was the mother of the poet’s daughter, Allegra, whom he often referred to as “it” or “my bastard”. Byron refused to receive Clare, not out of coldness but, on the contrary, because: “If I see her, it will result in another new relative.” Shelley’s own memories of Venice were more painful: his own daughter, Clara, died in the city after a brief illness. She is buried at the Lido. We tend to forget that even mythological figures such as Byron *et al.* were once fragile people made of flesh and blood. § Of women and Venice, Byron wrote: “A woman is virtuous here (according to the code) who limits herself to her husband and one lover. Those who have two, three or more are considered a little wild. But only those who are indiscriminate, diffuse or who form a low connection… are considered as overstepping the bounds of the modesty of marriage.” In another letter, he elaborates on his household expenses: “I have spent about five thousand pounds – & I needed not have spent one third of this – had it not been that I have a passion for women, which is expensive.” But he also felt that Venice’s disadvantages were “more than compensated by the sight of a single gondola emerging from the fog, or the Rialto bridge appearing round the corner.” § In May 1817, Byron attended a public execution in the city: “I saw three robbers guillotined… Two of these men behaved calmly enough, but the first of the three died with great terror and reluctance. He would not lie down; then the priest was obliged to drown his exclamations by still louder exhortations. The head was off before the eye could trace the blow. The pain seems little; and yet the effect to the spectator is very striking and chilling. The first made me shake so that I could hardly hold the operaglass (I was close, but determined to see, as one should, see everything, once, with attention); the second and third (which shows how dreadfully soon things grow indifferent), I am ashamed to say, had no effect on me as a horror, though I would have saved them if I could.” §

VENITIAN WEDDING
4038

Ott.re 16[illegible]

Del Banco

De 23. a 28. sett.re

Livorno

Ill.mo, et Ecc.mo Sig.r Sig.r Col.mo

Die 9 Augusti 1760

Recepte cum Verona adm. Dilco

Devendo restare esseguite le commiss.ni avvocantatemi in quelle dell'E.V.S. Ecc.ma p.p., fate ad ins.za della V. Comp.a del SS.mo Sacram.o nell'antica Parochiale di S. Severo di Bardolino, che commettono alli Leg.ti et Elletti di quella di S. Maria della Neve di d.o Loco non che alli s.ri Not.i di questa mia Canc.a à quali sono state esse let-tere intimate, la trasmessione costà delle sere esistenti p.tate e sequestrate nella già d.a Canc.a, riceverà perciò colle pnti V.E. sotto sigillo le medesime sere, consistenti in un Libro in folio, e ~~[illegible]~~ tre deci libreti, il che servirà per li effetti di giust.a, et in adempim.to de miei doveri bacciandole di cuo. le mani.

Vna li 8. Ag.o 1760.

Aluise Contarini p.mo Cap.o

159.

PUTTANA.

CORTEGIANE

Until 1950, there were twenty-five brothels in Venice. You will not find a single sex shop in Venice today and the recent Museum of Erotica has been roundly boycotted – in this respect, too, Venice is unique in Europe. But, oh the irony, for in far more prudish times than ours, Venice was home to all kinds of debauchery and depravity. § The city archives prove that La Serenissima regulated prostitution as early as 1443. Galleys were financed from the excise taxes levied on the exchange of money for sex. § In 1677, the poet and monk Jacques Boileau published *De l'abus des nudités de gorge*, a pamphlet warning against "abuses of the bosom". It cannot be a coincidence that he wrote his treatise after an extended sojourn in Venice. § The monk Fra Mauro issued his own condemnation from the pulpit in 1641: "*Sapine mulieres tan longas caudas investimentis habeant et per terram trahant qua res diablica est*" (the long train and the skirt are the devil!). § *Cortegiana* originally meant 'lady of the court', but that definition was soon subverted. The ever-pragmatic Venetians tended to present dowries only to the most beautiful girls in order to keep them out of prostitution – it was argued that they were far more likely to fall victim to temptation than their uglier counterparts, and that prostitutes indirectly helped to keep the wives of noblemen on their toes.

Venice has always been a city in which the extremes of life have effortlessly co-existed, such as decadence and chastity. If there is a separate word for gentlemen who have an affair with a nun – *muneghini* – then you know that it was not an isolated occurrence. In his *Dialogue*s, Aretino had the worldly-wise Nonna share her erotic past with the novitiate Antonia. It was the first book in the Christian world to be written in a popular, vulgar language. § According to eyewitnesses, the atmosphere in a Venetian convent was often a cross between the temple prostitution of antiquity and a medieval pleasure garden. In 1428, ten aristocratic lovers of Sister Filipa Barbarigo from the San Nicola Church on Torcello were prosecuted. And the notorious courtesan, Liseta de Buora, was a former nun at the convent of Sant'Angelo (which was closed down on the grounds of debauchery in 1474). In yet another cloister, a nun and an abbess duelled over their mutual lover. § Near the Fondamenta Savorgnan, in Cannaregio, there is a Jesuit church that once served as an asylum and shelter for the *percolanti*, or fallen women. They underwent a five-year rehabilitation programme. During this time they acquired a trade. Upon their release, they received a parting gift of clothes and household linen. § Charles de Brosses wrote in 1733: "In truth it would be to the nuns that I should most readily turn if I had to make a long stay here. All those I have seen through the grate at mass, chatting and laughing together so long as the service lasted, have struck me as good-looking and habited in such a way as to highlight their beauty. They have a charming little *coiffure* and a simple dress, but one that is of course perfectly white, revealing their shoulders and breasts to just the same degree as the dresses in the Roman style worn by our actresses." A meaningful comparison once you realise that the good people of the day did not rank actresses much higher than whores. § Venetian noblemen would often park their illegitimate daughters at the church and convent of San Zaccaria, under the direct protection of the Doge, where they would be raised as nuns. The Doge would visit once a year to "confess" and attend mass. In 864, a Doge was murdered during a banquet in his honour. § In Venice, as in Sicily, one sometimes encounters a heady mixture of piety and lust; for example, Santa Maria Formosa is Venetian dialect for 'Saint Mary the Voluptuous'. § Aretino wrote the 'instructive' handbook entitled *La vie des courtisanes*, which lists several categories of women: the *cortegiana di lume* (candlelight) was uglier and not as clean as the *cortegiana onesta*. § In the sixteenth century, the chronicler Marino Sanudo counted 11,654 registered prostitutes, although it goes without saying that the actual figure was probably much higher. At the 1509 census, Venice had 100,000 inhabitants, so this would have equated to 15% of the population. Back then, the authorities encouraged prostitution... as a way of promoting heterosexuality. Which is how the Ponte delle Tette acquired its official name. "Turkish whores dressed as men" also loitered around the Calle de le Turchette. Doge Sebastiano Venier defeated the Turks at the Battle of Lepanto and brought an entire harem of a hundred women back to Venice as the spoils of war. The Ponte de le Turchette was also the site of a "reform house for Turkish virgins". The most beautiful of them all, Selina, refused to marry a Turk, so he cut her throat. Despite the man's brother claiming they had left for their honeymoon, her skull was found hidden inside a case many years later. Even now, with her gaping wound, she haunts this world...

Because Venice is such a time capsule, it is easy to feel as though courtesans are spying on you or waiting just around the corner. Here are a few handy addresses for ladies of the night:

Lucia (in the alley next to Palazzo Corner)
Lucrezia (in Ca' Angeli, opposite Malipiero)
Giulia (in Calle Longa)
Nina (Ruga Giuffa, in San Zacharia).

All these courtesans have been dead for three hundred years, yet their aura still lingers.

Hotbeds of prostitution could also be found in Sant'Antonio ('behind the bridge'), San Giovanni in Bragora, on the Santa Trinita, on San Lio and in San Cassiano. The area around the Rialto was also a red-light district for a considerable period. And it is to the numerous prostitutes around the San Cassiano in San Polo, known as the *carampane*, that we owe the insult *vecchia carampana* (old whore). Carampane also boasted a notorious Turkish bath that led to the canal being nicknamed the *estufa* (the furnace). Cheap whores were recognisable by their yellow neckerchiefs. When the bell rang three times, they had to go inside, under penalty of a whipping. § In *Coryat's Crudities*, the Englishman Thomas Coryat described how seventeenth-century courtesans wore "many chains of gold and orient pearl like a second Cleopatra divers [sic] gold rings beautified with diamonds and other costly stones... A gown of damask – I speak this of the nobler courtesans – either decked with a deep gold fringe... or laced with five or six gold laces each two inches broad." And that such a prostitute will "endeavour to enchant thee, partly with her melodious notes that she warbles out upon her lute." He noted that most of the women were childless: "they have but a few, for according to the old proverb the best carpenters make the fewest chips." By way of a conclusion, he warns that many of the courtesans are "so loose that they are said to open their quivers to every arrow".

In 1543, the Council of Ten forbade prostitutes from wearing silk skirts and jewellery so as to avoid being mistaken for noblewomen – which happened all too often, apparently, and thus says something about the behaviour of aristocratic women. § In Renaissance times, a number of courtesans were so wealthy that they could afford to sponsor mass public entertainments. According to Michel de Montaigne, writing in 1580, many courtesans already owned palazzi: "I saw such a vast number of them, some hundred and fifty, spending money like princesses over furniture and attire, with no other source of income than the traffic aforesaid. Again, divers [sic] of the nobles of the city entertained courtesans at their own charges in the sight of everyone." While one could perhaps draw an analogy between courtesans and high-end call girls, I doubt there is a single escort in the world who can afford a palazzo in Venice. § In a letter dated 1580, included in *Il catalogo delle principali e piu onorate cortegiane di Venezia*, Veronica Franco, who never married, explains that the profession of courtesan is "hard enough to succeed in even if a woman has beauty, style, good judgment, and proficiency in many skills... It is a most wretched thing, contrary to human reason, to subject one's body and industriousness to a servitude whose very thought is most frightful. To become the prey of so many, at the risk of being despoiled, robbed, killed, deprived in a single day of all that one has acquired from so many over such a long time, exposed to many other dangers of receiving injuries and dreadful contagious diseases; to eat with another's mouth, sleep with another's eyes, move according to another's will, obviously rushing toward the shipwreck of one's mental abilities and one's life and body; What greater misery?" § Veronica herself was the daughter of a courtesan, so she was hardly unenlightened. She also had her portrait painted by Tintoretto, who was her lover for a time. The line between artist and whore was thin. Veronica Franco also published a collection of poems, *Terze Rime*, in 1575. During a banquet for Henri III in the Palazzo Ducale she was carried naked on a golden platter and recited her self-penned sonnets before the king. Just imagine the scene: a naked whore performing poetry for royalty or a president at a state banquet – which, in this day and age, is unthinkable. Franco almost ended up on the scaffold when she was accused of witchcraft by the Inquisition. Networking also existed back then, however, and she escaped the executioner thanks to her impeccable contacts. As recompense, she established a refuge for courtesans who wanted to leave the profession at the Fondamenta del Soccorso, near Santa Maria del Carmelo in 1590. Franco gave birth to six children, three of whom died in infancy. § In 1606, the Marquis of Ferrara was warned by the Marquise Bentivoglio: "I want you to promise me not to go to the women in Venice, because I have experienced how many of my acquaintances returned infected and then died because of that event." Up until the sixteenth and seventeenth centuries, it was not the plague but venereal disease that was the principal cause of death in Venice, and it claimed more lives than heart attacks, cancer, accidents and crime combined. Which is why well-bred mothers with randy sons who were desperate to learn the art of lovemaking preferred to pay for lessons from the daughters of impoverished nobles. § In 1780, William Beckford wrote to an English friend about Venice: "A thoughtless giddy transport prevailed; for, at this hour, anything like restraint seems perfectly out of the question; and however solemn a magistrate or senator may appear in the day, at night he lays up wig and robe and gravity to sleep together, runs intriguing about in his gondola, takes the reigning sultana under his arm, and so rambles half over the town, which grows gayer and gayer as the day declines. Many of the noble Venetians have a little suite of apartments in some out-of-the-way corner, near the grand piazza, of which their families are totally ignorant… Surely, Venice is the city in the universe best calculated for giving scope to the observations of a devil upon two sticks." § *Leggi e memorie Venete sulla prostituzione*, an informative guide from 1870, complete with prices and specialities, spans four hundred pages. § From all these chronicles we learn that courtesans had unusual beauty rituals: they applied raw veal to keep their skin supple and used urine to bleach their hair. They traditionally styled their tresses into two 'horns'. The painting *Parade of the Courtesans on the Rio della Sensa* depicts the evening ritual of the prostitutes who glided around in gondolas searching for clients. Until well into the eighteenth century, there was even an annual *Corso delle Cortegiane*: a kind of floating pageant during which a fleet of vessels, filled with the courtesans who were permitted to advertise in this manner, took to the water. § In the eighteenth century, Giorgio Baffo wrote numerous scabrous erotic poems about courtesans, some of which bear such subtle titles as *Inni alla mana* (Hymn to the vagina), *Lodi al culo* (Ode to the arse) and *Gusto di sborari* (The pleasure of ejaculation). § But traces of Venice's shady and sultry reputation existed well into the modern era. Daphne du Maurier used the expression 'Venetian tendencies' as a euphemism for lesbianism. And it is a historical fact that many homosexuals embarked on a Grand Tour only to settle in places such as Naples, Capri and Venice, this because homosexuality was a capital offence in Great Britain at the time. Not much earlier the very same was true of Venice: men found guilty of sodomy were hanged between the two columns in the Piazza San Marco before being set alight. In 1511, people even believed that an earthquake had been caused by "unnaturally sinful behaviour".

Walter Sickert painted *The Broken Prostitute*, a portrait of the Venetian whore Giuseppina. That the conservative and chaste reflexes of the Venetians led them to curse the morals of decadent tourists over the centuries is evident from the diaries of the diplomat Duff Cooper: "August 29, 1923… We went on the Piazza after dinner and were just too late to witness a scene in which a young American girl who is staying on the Lido was hissed and hooted and finally almost driven off the Piazza for being in an ordinary décolleté evening dress. A rather hostile crowd gathered round our party too, but they were soon moved off by the police." § Venice is awash with locations that are associated with myths and sagas related to sex and its heirs, lust and jealousy. The Casino degli Spiriti, the imposing, somewhat sinister house opposite San Michele, has over the centuries been the scene of orgies, adultery and duels between amorous rivals. The painter Giorgione is said to have died in the residence during an orgy in 1510. The house takes its name from the owner's wife, who saw her dead lover's ghost while keeping vigil. The servant who witnessed the apparition was driven to insanity. The only discernible contemporary allusion to prostitution seems to be the name of the string quartet that occasionally plays in Vivaldi's church: the Putana Veneziana. § Is Venice the perfect location for clandestine and torrid affairs? Is an ordinary relationship too banal for this setting? § In a way, Venice herself is like a faded courtesan who realises that her past will always appeal more to the imagination than her future.

Palazzo Cavalli.

VENEZIA — Rio del Pestrin.

22. VENEZIA — Rio Albrizzi. (Riproduzione vietata)
4 Juillet
Merci des bonnes nouvelles que j'ai reçues ce
matin samedi (1 lettre 1 carte

CORTE
DELL' ASTROLOGO
2048 – 2044

MORTE
A
VENEZIA

For an author, Venice is
the ideal place
in which to write
the final chapter of life.

It is not only *Death in Venice,*
both the book and film,
that suggests a connection between
La Serenissima and death.
The entire city radiates transience.
Certainly, out of season,
in misty October or icy February,
Venice is almost like a portal
to a parallel universe.

A gondola reminds one of Charon's boat, while the Grand Canal evokes the Styx. In autumn and winter, Venice is empty, desolate and mysterious, even sinister at times, and a palazzo will suddenly resemble a sepulchre or mausoleum, a flag will seem like a shroud, or a church recall a funerary chapel. § "In Venice, the will to live, the laws and rules as we know them, do not apply. It is a world of libertinage and spiritual drunkenness, where beauty does not seem to spring from life's impulses." But it was not only Thomas Mann whose melancholia intensified in Venice. August, Graf von Platen-Hallermünde, included the following line in his poem *Tristan*: "He who hath set his eyes on beauty has already committed himself to death". Henry James described Venice as "the most beautiful of tombs". At the same time, it is remarkable that a city in decay, in which everything is crumbling, eroding and sinking, can nevertheless exude a sense of immortality. § One reason for not swimming in the Lagoon is the fact that countless devotees of Venice (certainly not only Venetians) secretly have their ashes scattered over the water, thereby hoping to remain close to the city forever. § Its burial ground, San Michele, (which immediately reminds one of Böcklin's *Isle of the Dead*), was originally two separate islands until, in 1807, Napoleon had the dividing waterway filled in and converted the land into a public cemetery. Previously, it had been the exclusive resting place of the nobility and, earlier still, a prison. San Michele was once called the '*Cavana de Muran*' ('shelter for Murano'), although nobody knows why. § The Isle of the Dead has witnessed many dramas. It is where Fra Paolo Sarpi, who was stabbed to death, is buried. The poet Robert Browning died in Venice and, for a period, was laid out at San Michele. Harold Acton recalls that when Diaghilev died in Venice in 1929, Boris Koshno and a certain Lifar, who both considered themselves to be his closest companion, started a fight next to his corpse. "They literally rolled over the floor," Acton wrote in a letter. Roses and tattered ballet shoes are still left on Diaghilev's grave every day. Admirers and pilgrims place pens or pencils on the tombs of writers such as Joseph Brodsky and Ezra Pound. My heart bleeds for forgotten authors such as Rawdon Brown and G.P.R. James (his friends had the following optimistic but sadly unrealised epitaph engraved on his headstone: “His merits as a writer are known wherever the English language is, and as a man they rest on the heads of many. A few friends have erected this humble and perishable little monument.”) And my favourite grave – if one can say that – is dedicated to the life of a completely unknown and long since forgotten Miss Mitford (not the famous writer), who died here in 1885, on her honeymoon, barely twenty-four years old. § There are other cemeteries in Venice, often where you might least expect them: at the intersection of the Piscina San Samuele and the extension of the Fondamenta Narisi, you will find a tiny square on the left that, up until the seventeenth century, was an enormous plague pit. The small quadrangles next to a great many churches were once graveyards, as was the less well-known island of San Cristoforo. § Venice fosters the illusion that you can stop decay in its tracks, that it is not a perpetual and irreversible process after all, and that one can preserve the deteriorated, weathered and eroded city exactly as it appears today. § Bidding farewell to the splendour of Venice is a cruel and frustrating task, especially when you realise that even these worn and precarious stones will outlive you. On the other hand, if you are laid to rest in Venice, a resurrection is not a priority.

WARNER BROS présente
Un film de LUCHINO VISCONTI
MORT A VENISE
DIRK BOGARDE • BJORN ANDRESEN • SILVANA MANGANO
PANAVISION
TECHNICOLOR
LALANDE-COURBET 21 - WISSOUS

HOTEL
ROYAL DANIELI
VENEZIA

GRANDHÔTEL
VENISE
HOTEL
DANIELI ROYAL
EXCELSIOR
VENEZIA
CORSO
TRIESTE

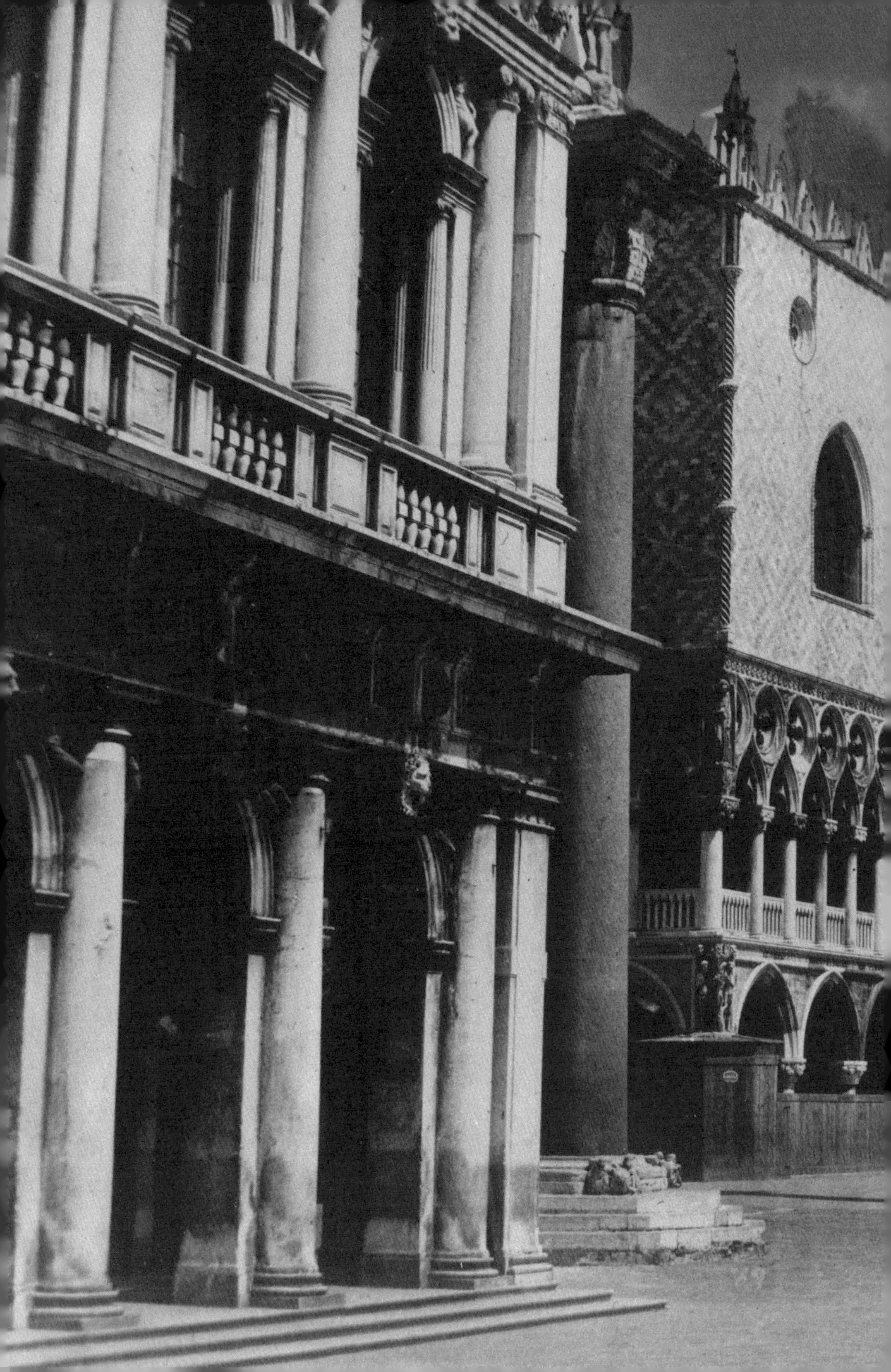

LA NOTTE

Venice possesses its own rhythm, its own unique way of keeping time. The night is also different in Venice. In these overcrowded times, the true Venice can only be experienced out of season, in the dead of night or at the crack of dawn. Between midnight and six o'clock in the morning it is not hard to imagine yourself back in 1654 or 1891. According to the Venetian calendar, which was in use until the eighteenth century, the New Year began on 1 March and sunset marked the start of each twenty-four hour period. § Nightfall strengthens the impression that a parallel world lurks just beneath the city's surface, a spectral realm that is even more mysterious than Venice by day. To borrow a painterly term, Venice is *sfumato*: hazy, blurred, rendered with vague outlines. Anything nebulous with the power to conceal – twilight, mist, fog – seems to have been created especially for La Serenissima. As you wander the streets, you feel as though you might suddenly discover, in every *sotoportego* (a narrow passageway between two houses with an arch, overhang or gate) or *ramo* (backstreet), a secret gate that leads to a hidden and even more magical city. The mist could be a portal to a hidden existence, and each canal a miniature Styx. Only after midnight does the Bridge of Sighs fulfil its promise. § Due to the lack of passion killers or other disturbances – cars and tourists – you often feel like an eavesdropper. Sirens wail throughout the night in New York, yet there is nothing to shatter the nocturnal illusion in Venice. Here, you can catch the authentic noises that would be drowned out in any other city: snippets of conversations, footsteps, echoes of children playing, the creak of a wooden bridge, a carpenter's scraping, the sound of water lapping against the side of a gondola... Venice awakens your inner voyeur: it is impossible not to stare when, at dusk, the lights are suddenly switched on in a palazzo. The only thing to avoid is sleepwalking: I know two Venetians who once sleepwalked into a canal. § Twinkling lights are more beautiful in Venice than anywhere else: flickering candles, torches or corner streetlamps cast grotesque shadows across the weather-beaten facades. Gaslight was not introduced to Venice until the end of the nineteenth century, which implies that the air was once thick with the smell of candles and spent wax coated the bridges and streets. Aesthetically speaking, one of the curses of the modern era is the cheap and cold neon light emitted by the trattorias. The nobility and merchants would have once employed a *codega*, a lantern bearer whose job it was to lead the way down the unlit alleyways and enliven the walk with interesting facts. § Nowhere does the past feel as close as it does in Venice. Not only are the previous centuries more tangible here than elsewhere, but because the city has barely been bombed or modernised (also a type of attack), it seems as if a host of illustrious protagonists from bygone days are waiting just around the corner. This is especially true when darkness falls. The tendency to describe Venice by night as a deserted film set speaks volumes about today's topsy-turvy world. We have become so indoctrinated that we see cultural imperialism (film, television) as the reality when the very opposite is true: Venice is real and a film is mere decor. § You wake up in the morning and realise with joyful amazement that Venice was not a dream. In winter, when the fog descends, or if you rise early enough, it seems as though Venice resurrects itself with every new day, as if the city shuns daylight and sinks just after sunset, or at least takes shelter. Venice at night is Venice for the initiated.

9

8693. P. Z. - VENEZIA.
CANAL GRANDE CON STA. MARIA DELLA SALUTE.

CAPTIONS

A photo from 1895 – a world without electricity, and thus also minus such annoyances as *vaporetti* and other types of noisy and polluting water traffic.

1889. The *felze*, a black cabin on a gondola, is a rare sight today. Not only did they offer protection against the heat, but also complete privacy.

The Danieli Hotel, then proudly called the 'Royal Danieli'. The welcome sign is an indication of the language spoken by the richest and most popular customers of the day.

The Rialto Bridge in 1891, before crude commercial shops marred the surroundings.

Photographs from 1891 by Ferdinando Ongania, the only professional photographer of his day who systematically documented the city and its inhabitants.

The birds in this photograph are fake, as they also are in many other views taken between 1880 and 1897. They were added by hand for the benefit of the tourists.

A zeppelin above the Lido in 1915.

The legendary Hotel Des Bains, which served as the backdrop for the film *Death in Venice*.

The Palazzo Vendramin, where Richard Wagner lived and died. It is now home to a casino.

The entrance to the Arsenale, where the Republic once built its warships. Part of the site is classified as a 'state secret' and is off limits to this very day.

From 1830, noble families who had fallen on hard times tended to rent their palazzi to the British and Americans who visited Venice on a Grand Tour of Europe. From the second half of the nineteenth century, these opulent residences started to be converted into hotels. Note the numerous heavy canopies that, in an era without air conditioning, were used to keep the interiors cool. The Excelsior Palace Hotel comes across as Moorish, medieval and Byzantine, but when it opened its doors in 1911 it was considered to be the height of glamour by the nouveau riche.

The Palazzo Contarini Minelli with the Scala del Bovolo, the so-called 'tower of the snail', built in 1499. Long a private residence, then a hotel and later a warehouse, it is now back in private ownership. It is where Orson Welles shot some of the scenes for his *Othello*.

The Palazzo Ducale. To look at the Doge's Palace is to cast your eyes upon the twelfth century. The original building was completely destroyed by fire in 963. The famous horses are the spoils of war and were transported to the city from Constantinople.

Photo from 1875. The square was not as empty as it seems, but the extremely long shutter speeds at the time ensured that anyone who moved was erased.

A unique sight that we may never see again due to global warming: the frozen Lagoon in 1929.

The 'cursed' Palazzo Dario (left).

Magic lanterns were the slides of the nineteenth century, hand-coloured and often falsified according to the wishes of the client: if 'Venice by night' or 'Venice in the snow' was requested, then the moon, night sky, sunset or a carpet of snow would be painted on top of a daytime image of the city. There was good reason for this: the shutter speeds were still very long and it was impossible to take pictures in the evening or in bad weather conditions.

"The pleasant intrigues and surprising adventures of an English nobleman at the last carnival of Venice", written by 'a person of quality' – the author of this scabrous account of the excesses during the carnival of 1707 wished to remain anonymous.

Letters written by Venetians in 1698 and 1760 respectively.

A now probably disappeared or secret theatre from the eighteenth century. Numerous palazzi remain in private hands and have not been restored since the nineteenth century. As a result, they have never been officially documented. An architect once told me: "Sometimes you find a chunk of stucco in the rubbish or a fragment of a fresco, which is a sure sign that there's something special behind those walls."

The *Bocca di Leone*, intended for the *denontie secrete.* Citizens could denounce alleged traitors of the Republic to the authorities by depositing an anonymous note in the lion's mouth, which naturally led to numerous abuses and false accusations. Translation of the text: "Secret denunciations against anyone who will conceal favours and services or will collude to hide the true revenue from them."

Photo from 1902, taken just after the collapse of the Campanile on the Piazza San Marco.
There is also a picture showing the actual moment it fell, but it is fake: the cracks and flying stones were later additions. Earlier, between 1548 and 1776, the Campanile, which was a much more impressive structure than the current tower, had been struck by lightning on so many occasions that people believed it was cursed.

A tip: 'Musica a Palazzo' is an organisation that arranges concerts in the Palazzo Barbarigo Minotto, which provides the perfect excuse for entering an authentic palazzo that is still in private hands (www.musicapalazzo.com).

DIETRO LE QUINTE

Concept & text: Serge Simonart

Images: Serge Simonart, drawn from his collection of ephemera and antiquarian books on Venice

Photos: Belga Image, Inge Bubbe, Attilio Codognato, Getty Image, Séverine Lacante, Mai image bank/ Sem Presser, Carlo Naya, Ferdinando Ongania, Reporters/Magnum Photos, Shutterstock, WikiArt, Serge Simonart, and dozens of anonymous artists and photographers working between 1860 and 1925

Photo editing: Séverine Lacante

Cover design: after 'Venezia' by Henriette 'Henry' Perl, a re-edition by Emil M. Engel, Vienna/Leipzig, 1895

Coordination: Hadewych Van den Bossche

Translation: Helen Simpson

Copy-editing: Derek Scoins

Design: Johan Jacobs & Serge Simonart

Art direction: Natacha Hofman

Printing: die Keure, Bruges

Binding: Brepols, Turnhout

ISBN 978 94 6388 750 2
D/2020/11922/17
NUR 653

Hannibal Books is part of Uitgeverij Kannibaal bv, Veurne, Belgium.

www.hannibalbooks.be

The author pays homage and extends his thanks to all those who have inspired and helped him: John Ruskin, Rolly Smeets, Charles Dickens, Harrison and Margaret Rhodes, André L'Hoëst, J.G. Links, Jan Morris, Chantal Pattyn, Wilfried Simonart, Astrid Verbeeck, Linnea Linderoth, Joanna Loonen, Julian Oscar Simeon, Elsje Helewaut, Chery Derycke, Brigitte Ghyselen, Alice Rees, Mario Fortuny, Daniela Ferretti, Marnix and Maja Neerman, John Julius Norwich, Donna Leon, Gianni Basso and Giacomo Casanova.

In January 2016, Klara presented a boxed set of CDs entitled *Venezia,* a musical journey through Venice selected by Serge Simonart. Published by Warner Music Benelux and also available on iTunes.

For my parents, who saw the light at a late age and became Venetians, so that their descendants can follow in their footsteps.

ANDATE IN PACE